D1385453

# *Austrian* cooking

## GRETEL BEER

Foreword by **Jennifer Paterson**

ANDRE DEUTSCH

First published in Great Britain in 1954 by André Deutsch Ltd

This edition first published in 1998 by André Deutsch Ltd
76 Dean Street
London W1V 5HA

www.vci.co.uk

André Deutsch is a VCI plc company

Printed and bound in Great Britain by St Edmundsbury Press, Suffolk

A catalogue record for this book is available from the British Library

ISBN 0 233 99471 8

Design by Kee Scott Associates

To Evelyn Forbes

## Grateful Acknowledgements

... to all members of my family who, for generations, noted and collected recipes: in neat books, full of asides and family gossip; on scraps of paper now yellowed with age; thin and spidery handwritings and bold ones written in indelible pencil; recipes passed on by word of mouth, altered and amended as the years went on and memories weakened. Grateful thanks to all of them... and to my husband who was never too surprised to test any samples that were going – no matter at what time of day or night they were proffered.

GB

# Contents

I'd like to explain 1

Soups and their Garnishes 4

Fish 26

Meat, Game and Poultry 32

Vegetables 64

Salads 75

Savoury Sauces 81

Dumplings and the Like 88

Desserts, Hot and Cold
including Sweet Sauces 96

Cakes, Pastries and Biscuits 126

Gateaux and Icings 190

Index 224

# *Austrian* cooking

## *Foreword*

Gretel Beer's *Austrian Cooking* has stood the test of time. During the forty-four years since the book was first published it has never been out of print. Some receipts may be politically incorrect but that endears the book to me. An amazing one for 'Lights' is a must for the uninitiated. I thought lights were for dogs but that is just an English bit of bigotry I'm sure. I shall try it – if I can find the lights – they may be a little difficult to buy here!

There is, of course, a receipt for Sachertorte. It is not a favourite of mine, but most, or at least half of the book is dedicated to cakes, pastries and biscuits that are rip-roaringly fattening, and to delicious sweetmeats. For soup lovers there is plenty to choose from and there is a very good chapter on fish. Although Mrs Beer's excellent receipts are mostly for river fish like pike and carp, which are tricky if you don't come across them often, she does suggest that the methods are suitable for cod and haddock too.

Try out some of the more unusual receipts and enjoy!

Jennifer Paterson

# *Austrian* cooking

# *Introduction to 1998 Edition*

Rationing was still with us when I wrote *Austrian Cooking* – to be abolished just before publication – but I was not prepared to make concessions to quality. Substitutes were definitely 'out'. I advocated making your own cream cheese, gave instructions on how to siphon the cream off the milk, was mean with meat portions and relentlessly halved quantities for rich Torten – better a smaller cake and the real thing than the mockery of synthetic second-best. I used fresh herbs – some of which, like dill, were practically unknown in this country and vanilla pods were stuck firmly into jars of sugar, just to forestall any idea of synthetic flavourings.

The book has remained unchanged throughout the forty-four years since it was first published – no alterations or amendments were made to later editions either in this country or abroad (not even in a much-treasured German translation). In fact the only changes I have made in this new edition were to correct a few mistakes which had gone unnoticed for forty-four years – like larding a saddle of hare twice – no doubt missing a few more and adding some in doing so. And to add metric measurements I went back to my original family recipes, particularly for cakes and puddings, which were of course metric in the first place and more precise. Of course you know that you should follow either metric or imperial in the same recipe – mixing the two is counter-productive, like trying to write on both sides of the paper at the same time…

Some of the recipes are easier to accomplish now. There were no food processors then – no foil or clingfilm either – the first electric mixers had just made their appearance and everything had to be puréed or creamed by hand (and some of it all the better for it). Flour was either plain or self-raising – which no respecting Austrian cook would use. ('Only lazy cooks use baking powder.' I was told by a great pastry cook, 'You rely on well-creamed butter and sugar, whipped egg whites and the like for lightness.') You can now choose from different kinds of flour – even the special flour for making pasta is now available – but as a rule of thumb it is still plain flour, with strong flour for anything made with yeast. And I still advocate using fresh yeast (if you use dried yeast the quantities will have to be varied) simply because there is nothing to beat the scent of fresh yeast ripening in a warm kitchen with the winter winds howling outside.

Eggs are now sized – use large eggs unless otherwise stated – and I am now compelled to add the warning that 'raw or semi-cooked eggs (as advocated in some recipes) should not be fed to the very young, frail or elderly.' I hope I am not breaking the law by saying that I have eaten these dishes throughout my life, thus qualifying under the first as well as the last category, without coming to any harm. But then I've always believed in living dangerously (like cooking a delicate cream over direct heat and not in a double boiler).

Whilst all ingredients were available – though some in short supply – when the book was first published in 1954, this is not now the case. You can't find a boiling fowl – or mutton – at least not without some considerable effort – and at present the sale of beef on the bone – and some offal – is allowed only for feeding animals. Should it be used for human consumption, the butcher is liable to be prosecuted. Perhaps this the reason why my Dachshund is in frequent negotiation with his butcher...

I suppose to bring the book really up-to-date I should report the final chapter of the Demel v Sacher war of the cakes: Sacher won. ('He'll go to hell for this and be boiled in a vat of hot chocolate,' said a stalwart Demel waitress about the owner of Sacher when the judgement was made.) No doubt the war continues on the other side where the erstwhile owners of Sacher and Demel now preside over a heavenly range of Viennese delicacies – a small selection of which I hope will find favour with you from this book.

Gretel Beer
London, July 1998

The culinary bouquet of Austria is made up of many fragrances. Of sugar and butter and rum. Of toasted almonds and chestnuts roasting at street corners. Of new wine and old love for recipes passed from mother to daughter. Of fresh coffee and comfortable gossip. Of sweet whipped cream and a leisurely contemplation of life. Of freshly scrubbed wooden tables and mounds of yeast dough rising in deep bowls. Of strong beer and Gulasch spiced with caraway seeds. But above all, of love for good food and the spirit of adventure that goes into its making.

The culinary flavour of Austria is a gentle flavour. It knows of the fiery spices of Hungary and the elegance of French cuisine. It derives much of its strength from Moravia and much of its daring from Poland. It is a broadminded flavour – if flavours can be broadminded – a flavour that knows the meaning of compromise...

Gretel Beer
1954

# *I'd like to explain*

## *About flour*

In Austria one differentiates between *glattes* and *griffiges* flour, a distinction unknown here. Use plain white flour throughout, unless otherwise stated, keep it dry and sift before use.

## *About sugar*

Most Austrian cake recipes, etc. call for icing sugar. Castor sugar or granulated sugar can be used, but the mixture will be slightly coarser. If you have to use granulated or castor sugar where it is a question of creaming butter and sugar, add a drop of hot water towards the end of the creaming process. This is particularly important for all types of butter-cream fillings, etc.

## *About butter*

A great many Austrian recipes are based on butter and the very flavour it imparts to a dish. For that reason you will find the words 'butter or margarine' used only rarely in the book. Of course you can use margarine, though I personally would never substitute it for butter in any kind of cream filling and the like. If you do make cakes and pastries with margarine, spare enough butter for the cake tin — it makes a world of difference.

## *About brushing over pastry with egg or milk or melted butter*

For small pastries an ordinary pastry brush is too heavy. In Austria long goose feathers — cleaned and tied into small bundles — are used. Worth remembering next time you buy a goose. Alternatively, use a small paint brush and keep the pastry brush for 'heavy' jobs.

## *About whisking egg whites*

A pinch of icing sugar added when whisking them is as good as the proverbial and often quoted pinch of salt. Better, in fact, when making cakes.

# *Austrian* cooking

## About cream

This is an essential part of Austrian cookery and 'mock' cream will not do. At the time of writing, supplies of cream are plentiful – alternatively I simply syphon the cream off the top of my full cream milk with an eye-dropper or a fountain-pen filler or with a special gadget bought for 2s. You can collect quite a lot that way – and I do not take *all* the cream off my milk, always leaving about 6mm (1/4in) at the top. Thick sour milk or yoghurt can be used to replace sour cream in soups, sauces, stews and cakes.

## About flavourings

Steer clear of synthetic flavourings. A few drops of lemon or orange juice, or rum or real fruit syrup are no more expensive and infinitely better than all the synthetic flavourings in the world. And keep a vanilla pod with some of your icing sugar (referred to as vanilla sugar throughout the book).

## About cream cheese

Pour your sour milk into a bowl. When it is really thick hang it up in a cheesecloth or clean tea towel. The moisture will drip out gradually and you will be left with what is called *Topfen* in Austria. I have referred to it as cream cheese throughout the book and it is used for many recipes, mainly sweet ones.

## About adding rum to pastries which are fried

This is essential, as it stops the pastry from absorbing too much fat while frying.

## About horseradish

Quite a number of recipes in this book call for it. It is a longish root which can be bought at most greengrocers'. Keep it in water and grate off as much as is required (having scraped it clean first). Grate rather coarsely. Incidentally, it will make you cry a little, like onions.

## About fat

Keep the various kinds of dripping well apart. Trim the fat off too-fat pork, cut it into cubes and render it down.

# I'd like to explain

## About tough meat

A mallet for beating meat is one of the most useful kitchen utensils and no Austrian cook would dream of being without it. The back of a knife is acceptable as a substitute – mark the meat with a criss-cross pattern. And a sprinkling of lemon juice will also help to break down tough fibres.

## About pre-heating of oven

Should be done always. Essential for soufflés, cakes, and most pastries.

## About the selection of recipes

The culinary repertoire of Austria is curiously proportioned. A strict sufficiency of necessities and a rich abundance of all that is sweet and slightly extravagant – facts which had to influence my choice of recipes for this book.

*Austrian* cooking

# Soups and their Garnishes

# Soups and their Garnishes

In Austria a line is drawn between *echte Suppen* ('real' soups based on stock made from fish or meat or at least bones) and *falsche Suppen* ('phoney' soups based mainly on vegetable stock with quite often a meat cube or two added). This distinction does not reflect on the quality of *falsche Suppen*, which are usually very good. It is made simply to get one's sense of culinary values right from the start, and to impress once and for all the fundamental seriousness of stock. Stock may be made of many things: beef bones or veal bones or the water in which a piece of bacon was cooked. It may be made of *Bratensaft* (gravy minus the fat, plus any scrapings left in the baking dish after roasting some meat) or a small portion of left-over goulash. It can be vegetable stock or an honest beef cube dissolved in hot water. But it should never come out of a stock-pot which has been kept simmering for days, adding bits of this and bits of that!

*Austrian* cooking

# Clear Beef Broth

*Klare Rindsuppe*

The best clear beef broth is one which has had more than a nodding acquaintance with a piece of beef as well as with some beef bones. This is not an extravagance, because there is no kinder (and more economical) treatment for a tough piece of meat than to simmer it slowly, with plenty of vegetables, and thereby transform it into what is known in Austria as *gekochtes Rindfleisch*. (In restaurants it usually appears as *gekochtes Rindfleisch, fein garniert*, which is the boiled beef sliced, served with 5 or 6 different vegetables and usually also chive or dill sauce.) It really works both ways, you get plenty of good soup, tender, luscious meat (with no shrinkage in cooking) and all that with a minimum of trouble. No wonder the Austrians set such store by their *gekochtes Rindfleisch* that they even select the better cuts of meat for that purpose. Thus they will make their choice between *Hieferschwanzl* and *Tafelspitz*, classed as *Gustostueckl'n* in Austria (specially delectable cuts), as well as *Kruspelspitz, Kavalierspitz* and *Dicker Spitz*... Alas and alack, we shall probably have to be satisfied with a shin of beef (commonly known in Austria as *Wadschunken*).

Before starting you will have to decide whether you want to make what is known as *weisse Rindsuppe* (white beef broth, though its colour is really golden yellow) or *braune Rindsuppe* (brown beef broth). For the latter, vegetables and bones (this is important) must be browned first in a little fat. Any surplus fat must be poured away and only then are water and meat added. If you have only a small piece of meat it is better to aim at brown beef broth as the initial browning of bones and vegetables brings out a fuller flavour and you may also add a beef cube towards the end of the cooking time.

Having thus made your decision, you begin by preparing your vegetables. For about ½–3/4kg (1–1½lb)) of meat you need about two carrots, one large onion, two leeks, a turnip, 1 or 2 tomatoes, a celeriac or a stick of celery (the stringy part), some parsley (including roots) and about ½kg (1lb) of beef bones chopped into convenient pieces, salt and a few peppercorns. A few sprigs of cauliflower may also be added. Wash and clean vegetables, cut onion into quarters, break tomatoes into halves. Scald bones and rinse in cold water. Wipe meat with a cloth wrung out in hot water. Put everything in a large saucepan, cover with about 2 litres (3–3½ pints) of water and bring to boil. Lower the flame immediately and simmer very slowly until meat is tender. This takes about 2 to 3 hours. If bones only are used, simmer a little longer. Do not let it boil and *do not remove* any scum which may rise to the top. If you have plenty of bones and want to preserve the full flavour of the meat you may prefer to add the meat only when the water has reached boiling point and then lower heat immediately. Personally, I do not advocate this. I must admit that it improves the flavour of the meat, but this improvement is in my opinion slight and the loss of flavour as far as the soup is concerned infinitely greater. When the meat is tender, lift out carefully, keep hot (preferably over steam) with a little of the soup poured over. Strain soup, leave to cool a little, then remove excess fat.

Straining through a fine sieve or clean tea towel (previously wrung out in cold water) may suffice, but for really clear soup follow the recipe overleaf:

*Austrian* cooking

# To Clear Soup

Have ready some crushed eggshells and one eggwhite. Whisk crushed eggshells (yes, it can be done) and eggwhite lightly with ½ cup of dry white wine (or about the same quantity of cold water and a little lemon juice) and 1 cup of the soup, then stir carefully into boiling strained soup. Lower heat immediately and leave over lowest possible flame for another 15 minutes and you will find that all impurities have sunk to the bottom of the saucepan, together with the eggshells. Strain off soup carefully. (There is another way of clearing soup – and jelly – too, which involves the use of fresh prime beef. We shall not go into that, however.)

In Austria all soups consisting of clear beef broth plus an addition such as noodles, etc., are named after that addition. Thus you will find *Schoeberlsuppe* (clear beef broth with *Schoeberl*) or *Leberknoedelsuppe* (clear beef broth with liver dumplings), etc. The recipes on the following seven pages are all for such additions and there is no hard and fast rule as to whether they should be used with white or brown broth. Some of these *Suppeneinlagen* (as they are called in Austria) are of course so simple that they require no recipe – a little semolina sprinkled into the soup, or rice, or barley. Then there are *Fritatten*, which are ordinary pancakes (unsweetened of course) cut into thin strips and dropped into the hot soup just before serving. And then there is *Bouillon mit Ei,* which I value above all others. I believe that it is the best tonic after a tiring (and trying) day, with the possible exception of *Fernet Branca* (which I swear cures most ills). To make *Bouillon mit Ei* (clear beef broth with egg) you need one egg (or egg yolk) per person as well as the clear beef broth. Slip an egg yolk (or egg) on each soup plate and then pour the hot soup over. That is all. The heat from the soup just sets the outer 'layer' of the egg and you stir it into the soup as you eat it.

Here, then, are a few more additions for your clear soup:

# 'Fried Peas'

*Backerbsen*

| | |
|---|---|
| 1 egg | Salt |
| 2 tablespoons milk | Fat or oil for frying |
| 45g (1 1/2oz) flour | |

Prepare a batter with the above ingredients; the mixture should be of thick, running consistency. Have ready a pan of smoking hot fat, about 2cm (3/4in) deep. Holding a ladle in one hand, pour the batter through a sieve with large holes (or a perforated spoon) into the hot fat. Fish out as soon as the little 'peas' are golden brown, place on kitchen paper to drain and keep hot. Hand separately with clear bouillon.

There is another and more thrifty way of preparing these little 'peas'. When making Strudel, keep the pastry trimmings. Cut out tiny rounds (we always used a thimble) and drop into smoking hot fat. Fry until golden brown and serve as above.

# Savoury Squares

*Biscuit Schoeberl*

*Schoeberl* are a typically Austrian addition to clear bouillon. They are usually baked in a special tin (*Schoeberlpfanne*), cut into squares when cold and reheated in the oven just before serving. Any cake tin is of course quite satisfactory, though a square one is preferable, but the mixture should not be spread higher than about the thickness of a finger.

| | | |
|---|---|---|
| 1 egg | 25g (1oz) flour | Pinch salt |

Separate egg yolk and whites. Whisk egg white with a pinch of salt until stiff, fold into lightly whisked yolk. Fold in flour. Spread on a buttered and floured baking tin, bake at 180°C/350°F/Gas 4 until golden brown (about 15 minutes). Cool on a rack, cut into squares when cold and reheat just before seeing. Hand separately on a warmed plate or add to clear bouillon just before serving.

# Small Butter Dumplings

*Butternockerl*

60g (2oz) butter
1 egg

90g (3oz) flour
Pinch salt

Cream butter, add egg and flour alternately. Salt to taste. Cover bowl and leave to stand for about 15 to 30 minutes. Cut small balls with the help of a teaspoon and drop into boiling soup. As soon as mixture has been used up, lower flame and leave to simmer for about 15 minutes.

# Eingetropftes

1 egg
About 50–60g (2oz) flour

Pinch salt

Mix flour, salt and egg to a smooth batter (exact amount of flour naturally depends on size of egg). Pour batter through a funnel into boiling soup. Leave to rise once, then remove soup from heat and serve straight away.

# Cheese Slices

*Kaeseschnitten*

1 tablespoon butter
1 scant tablespoon flour
4 tablespoons milk
2 tablespoons grated Parmesan
  or Cheddar cheese
2 tablespoons grated Edam cheese

1 egg
Salt, pepper
Grated Cheddar cheese for
  sprinkling over top
Rolls

Melt butter, stir in flour. Cook gently, do not brown. Gradually add milk, salt and pepper. Remove from fire, stir in cheese and finally the egg. Cut rolls into slices the thickness of a finger and spread thickly with this mixture. Sprinkle with cheese. Brown quickly in very hot oven and hand separately with clear bouillon.

The cheese mixture can be prepared beforehand and the slices just popped into the oven at the last minute.

# Liver Dumplings

*Leberknoedel*

150g (5oz) liver
2 rolls
30g (1oz) dripping or butter
1 egg
1 tablespoon chopped parsley

60g (2oz) breadcrumbs
1 tablespoon flour
Salt, pepper
1 small onion

Soak rolls in water or milk, squeeze out moisture. Mince liver and rolls finely. Chop onion. Melt dripping (or butter), fry onion and parsley lightly. Remove pan from fire, stir in liver, add minced rolls, egg, flour, salt, pepper and breadcrumbs. Salt and pepper to taste. Leave for 15 minutes. Form small balls – about 2.5cm (1in) in diameter – and drop into boiling soup. Lower flame and simmer gently for 15 to 20 minutes.

# Small Liver Dumplings

*Lebernockerln*

150g (5oz) liver
3 rolls
30g (1oz) dripping or butter
Salt

1 egg
4 tablespoons flour
1 small onion
1 tablespoon chopped parsley

Soak rolls in water or milk, squeeze out moisture. Mince liver and rolls finely. Chop onion. Melt butter, fry onion and parsley lightly. Remove pan from fire, stir in liver, salt, add minced rolls, egg and flour. Salt and pepper to taste. Scoop out small balls with a teaspoon and drop into boiling soup. Lower flame and simmer gently for about 15 minutes.

*Austrian* cooking

# *Leberreis*

Prepare mixture for *Lebernockerln* as above. Holding a large-holed grater or perforated spoon in one hand, force mixture through the holes with the help of a palette knife, so that it drops into the boiling soup in the shape of small rice kernels. Cook for a few minutes only.

# Savoury Strudel *(For Clear Soup)*

*Lungenstrudel*

Strudel pastry (see page 159)
  using 200g (6oz) flour only
150g (5oz) lights
1 small onion

1 egg yolk
30g (1oz) butter or dripping
Chopped parsley
Salt, pepper, caraway seeds

Clean lights and cook in salt water. Chop onion and fry lightly in butter or dripping, together with the chopped parsley. Salt, pepper and caraway seeds to taste. Add chopped lights, toss in hot butter or dripping, then remove from fire and bind with the egg yolk. Pull out strudel pastry as described on page 159. Spread filling over two-thirds of the pastry, roll up as for Swiss roll. Secure ends, then make indentations about 5cm (2in) apart with the handle of a wooden cooking spoon. Cut into slices where marked and drop into boiling soup. Cook for about 10 to 15 minutes. Alternatively, roll complete strudel in a well-buttered tea towel, twist ends and tie well, then cook in boiling soup for 15 minutes. Remove towel, cut strudel into convenient slices and serve in hot bouillon.

    *Fleischstrudel* is made in exactly the same way, using cooked meat instead of lights.

# *Small Semolina Dumplings*

*Griessnockerl*

| | |
|---|---|
| 1 tablespoon lard or butter | 4 tablespoons coarse semolina |
| 1 egg | Pinch salt |

Cream butter or lard, gradually add salt, semolina and egg. Leave for 1 hour. With the help of a teaspoon, scoop out small balls and drop into boiling soup. Lower flame as soon as all the mixture has been used and simmer gently for about 15 to 20 minutes.

# *Small Marrow Dumplings*

*Mark Knoederl*

| | |
|---|---|
| 100g (3¹/₂oz) breadcrumbs | 1 egg |
| About 140ml (¹/₄ pint) milk | Salt, pepper |
| 100g (3¹/₂oz) bone marrow | Chopped parsley |

Crush bone marrow lightly, place in a bowl over steam to soften. It should melt, but not get really hot (in Austrian culinary language this is called *zerschleichen*). Moisten breadcrumbs with the milk, and salt and pepper to taste. Add softened marrow, salt, pepper, chopped parsley and finally the egg. Work well together, adding a little more breadcrumbs if necessary. Leave for 30 minutes, form small dumplings and drop into boiling soup. Simmer for 15 minutes.

# *Reibgerstl*

For this you can use the trimmings from strudel pastry or any paste left after making noodles. Alternately, make a very firm paste with 1 egg, salt and about 100g (3¹/₂oz) flour. Pat into a round and leave to dry, then grate on a coarse grater. Dry in the oven on a baking sheet, then sprinkle into boiling soup and cook for a few minutes.

*Austrian* cooking

# Meat Turnovers

*Schlick Krapfen*

### Paste

*1 egg*
*1 tablespoon butter*
*150g (5¹/2oz) flour*
*Salt*

### Filling

*200g (7oz) cooked meat*
*1 egg*
*Salt, pepper*
*50g (2oz) dripping*
*1 small onion*
*1 tablespoon parsley*

Sift flour and salt, make a little well in centre and drop in the egg. Cut butter into small pieces and mix everything to a soft paste, using a knife for the first stage of the mixing, then knead well. Divide paste into two parts, sprinkle with a litte flour and leave for 30 minutes. In the meantime prepare filling by mincing the meat finely. Chop onion and fry in dripping, add parsley and minced meat. Salt and pepper to taste. Remove from fire, stir in egg. Roll out paste thinly, place small dabs of the filling within 2.5cm (1in) of pastry edge, about two fingers apart. Brush round filling with egg white or milk, fold over edge. Cut into semicircles with a pastry cutter. Repeat procedure until all the pastry has been used. Drop into boiling salt water and cook gently for about 15 minutes. Drain and serve in clear bouillon.

# Noodles for Soup

*Suppennudeln*

*125g (4oz) flour*
*Pinch salt*

*1 egg*
*1 tablespoon water*

For making noodles, strudel pastry, etc., you should have a wooden pastry board. Sift flour and salt, make a small well in centre, drop in egg and water. Stir flour in with a knife, then knead well. Pat into a round, then roll out thinly. Leave to dry for about 30 minutes. Cut into strips, about 7.5cm (3in) wide. Place strips on top of each other, cut into very thin strips. Leave to dry on the pastry board, then cook as and when required.

# 'Little Patches' (Small Pasta Squares)

*Fleckerl*

Prepare dough as described for Noodles. Cut into strips about the width of a finger, then heap on top of each other. Cut into squares. Dry and use as above.

# Vegetable Soup

*Fruehlingssuppe*

This soup should be made with the freshest of young vegetables. Peas, young carrots, a small cauliflower broken into sprigs, beans and – if possible – 1 or 2 kohlrabi cut into small cubes. For 1.5 litres (3 pints) of soup you need about 450g (1lb) vegetables. Toss vegetables, which should be cut into cubes, etc., of similar size, in about two tablespoons butter for a few minutes. Cover with a lid and simmer for another 5 minutes, then pour on 1.5 litres (3 pints) clear beef broth (see page 6). Cook until vegetables are tender – no longer. Adjust seasoning and serve.

# Soup made with Roe

*Fischbeuschelsuppe*

450g (1lb) roes, skinned
Bay leaf
3 peppercorns
1 onion
Thyme
Celery

Dash vinegar
2 tablespoons butter
2 tablespoons flour
Pinch sugar
Salt

Cook bay leaf, peppercorns, onion, thyme and celery in about 1 litre (2 pints) water for 30 minutes. Melt butter, add skinned roes, cover with lid and simmer gently until roes are cooked. Lift out carefully, stir flour into melted butter and brown lightly. Gradually add strained vegetable stock, vinegar and a little sugar. Cut roes into cubes, add to soup and serve with fried croutons.

Although *Beuschel* usually refers to lights, in the case of *Fischbeuschel* it simply means hard roe. In Austria the most frequently used are roes of carp or pike.

# Goulash Soup

*Gulasch Suppe*

This is really a meal in itself, fully deserving a good portion of meat. You can 'stretch' the meat if need be, replacing part of the quantity by a pair of Frankfurter sausages, cut into slices.

3 large onions
Fat for frying
1 tablespoon paprika
1 teaspoon salt
Caraway seeds

250g (1/2lb) beef (shin for preference)
1 tablespoon tomato purée
3 large potatoes
Dash vinegar

Cut beef into small cubes. Slice onion finely. Fry onion in fat until golden brown, add paprika, salt, caraway seeds and vinegar. Add meat, stir once, then add tomato purée. Continue stirring until nicely browned, then add water to cover. Simmer very slowly for 20 minutes, then add potatoes cut into small cubes. Simmer until potatoes are soft. Adjust seasoning, add a little more water if necessary.

A small quantity of left-over goulash (see page 40) may also be used for making Goulash Soup: Warm the goulash carefully, so that it does not burn, then add sufficient hot stock (or water and stock cube) to give the required quantity. Add some cubed potatoes and some sliced Frankfurter sausages and cook until potatoes are soft. Adjust seasoning.

# Calf's Head Soup

*Kalbskopfsuppe*

| | |
|---|---|
| 1/4 calf's head | Salt, peppercorns |
| 100g (3oz) mushrooms | 1 onion |
| 100g (3oz) butter | 1 large carrot |
| 60g (2oz) flour | Bay leaf |
| A little lemon juice | 1 tablespoon chopped parsley |

Scald calf's head with boiling water, rinse with cold water. Set to cook with salt, a few peppercorns, onion, carrot and bay leaf, taking care that it should be completely covered with water while cooking. Cook until calf's head is soft. Clean and slice mushrooms. Melt butter, add sliced mushrooms and a little lemon juice. Simmer in covered saucepan until mushrooms are cooked. Dust with flour, stir, then gradually add the strained stock. Simmer for another 5 minutes, then add calf's head cut into strips and finely chopped parsley.

*Austrian* cooking

# Soup made with Split Peas

*Erbsenpureesuppe*

250g (1/2 lb) split peas
Stock (see below)
1 large onion
2 carrots
2 rashers bacon
A little sugar

300ml (1/2 pint) milk (as much 'top' as possible)
Bay leaf, thyme
1 tablespoon flour
Salt, pepper

The best stock to use is the water in which some ham or gammon has been cooked. In fact in Austria the boiling of a ham or a piece of smoked pork is almost invariably followed by split pea soup. Let the stock get cold, take off all the fat. If the bacon or the gammon was very salty, cook two large raw potatoes with the peas — to be thrown away before the soup is passed through the sieve. Soak peas overnight. Pour away the water in the morning. Cut the bacon into small cubes, slice the onion finely. Melt bacon in a thick saucepan, fry sliced onion in the fat until golden brown. Add the peas, carrot, salt (if necessary) or the potatoes, a little pepper, sugar, thyme and bay leaf. Cover with stock and simmer very gently until the peas are soft, then pass everything through a sieve. Slake the flour with a little of the milk, add to hot soup and cook for another 10 minutes. Adjust seasoning, add remainder of milk and simmer gently for 10 minutes. Serve with fried croutons, or small pieces of sausage heated in the soup, or both. A small piece of butter stirred into the soup just before serving is a good thing.

# Cream of Lentil Soup

*Linsenpureesuppe*

250g (1/2lb) brown lentils
2 large potatoes
1 carrot
1 onion
1 tablespoon flour
1 heaped tablespoon butter
  or dripping

Lemon juice
1 bay leaf
Thyme
Salt, pepper
1 scant litre (1 1/2 pints) water
1 ham bone or bacon rinds

Wash lentils and soak overnight in cold water. Wash again, then drain in a sieve. Slice onion and carrot, toss in hot butter or dripping until lightly browned. Add lentils, stir, then dust with flour. Brown lightly, add water, salt, pepper, thyme, bay leaf, sliced potatoes and ham bone (or bacon rinds). Cook until lentils are quite soft (about 2 to 2 1/2 hours). Remove bay leaf and ham bone, pass everything through a sieve. Return to stove, add a little lemon juice, adjust seasoning and serve with fried croutons. A little yoghurt stirred in just before serving (or 2 tablespoons top milk) greatly improves the flavour.

# *Austrian* cooking

# Cream of Game Soup

*Wildpureesuppe*

| | |
|---|---|
| 350g (³/4lb) game (weighed without bones) | 1 bay leaf |
| 175g (6oz) chestnuts | 1 small onion |
| 1 tablespoon butter | Parsley |
| 1 tablespoon flour | Dash brandy |
| A small knob butter | 1 carrot |
| Salt, pepper, nutmeg | Small piece celery |

Make an incision across top of chestnuts, cook in water until soft. Remove skins and pass chestnuts through sieve while still hot. Cut meat into convenient pieces. Melt butter, add sliced carrot, onion, celery and parsley. Toss in butter until very lightly browned. Add meat, stir and add salt, pepper and nutmeg. Add bay leaf and chestnuts and sufficient water to prevent burning. Cover with a lid and simmer until meat is soft. Remove onion and bay leaf, pass everything through a sieve. Return to stove, add 1 1/2 litres (2 1/2 pints) water and simmer for another 15 minutes. Slake flour with a little water and add to hot soup. Cook for 5 more minutes, adjust seasoning and stir in a knob of butter and the brandy just before serving.

# Caraway Soup

*Kuemmelsuppe*

| | |
|---|---|
| 100g (3oz) dripping or butter | Salt, pepper |
| 100g (3oz) flour | Fried croutons |
| 1³/4 litres (3 pints) water | 2 beef cubes |
| 1 tablespoon caraway seeds | |

Melt dripping or butter. Stir in flour and fry until golden brown. Add caraway seeds, salt and pepper to taste. Gradually stir in water, add beef cubes and simmer for 20 to 25 minutes. Hand fried croutons separately.

# Bread Soup

*Panadlsuppe*

| | |
|---|---|
| 2 day-old bread rolls | Salt, pepper |
| 1 scant litre (1 1/2 pints) clear stock | 1 egg yolk |
| (preferably from veal bones) | 1/2 cup cream |
| Chopped chives | |

Cut rolls into cubes and cook with the stock until rolls have been completely absorbed by soup. Salt and pepper to taste. Whisk egg yolk with cream, gradually pour on the hot soup whisking all the time. Sprinkle with chives and serve at once. A small lump of butter added just before serving greatly improves the flavour.

# Potato Soup

*Erdaepfelsuppe*

| | |
|---|---|
| 1 large carrot | 1 onion |
| Fresh parsley | Salt, pepper, marjoram |
| 1 small celeriac | Fat for frying |
| 1 clove garlic | 1 tablespoon flour |
| 1 tomato | 1 1/8 litres (2 pints) stock (beef |
| 6 large potatoes | or veal) |

Peel potatoes, cut into small cubes. Add to stock, together with crushed clove of garlic, sliced carrot, celeriac, parsley and tomato. Simmer until potatoes are very soft, then push everything through a sieve. Salt, pepper and marjoram to taste. Slice onion, brown in fat, dust with flour and stir. Add soup gradually, stir in a little more stock if necessary. Simmer for another 10 minutes before serving. Sprinkle with chopped parsley. Alternatively, cut two medium potatoes into cubes and cook in soup until soft but not 'mushy'.

# Semolina Soup

*Geroestete Griess Suppe*

1 1/2 litres (2 1/2 pints) stock
60g (2oz) coarse semolina
1 heaped tablespoon good
  dripping or butter

Salt, pepper
Chopped chives

Melt dripping or butter, add semolina and brown lightly. Gradually add stock and cook gently for about 30 minutes. Salt and pepper to taste. Serve sprinkled with chopped chives. There are numerous versions and improvements to this particular soup – sliced mushrooms may be added to the stock, or it can be bound with an egg yolk in the usual way just before serving. It is a good soup, a quick soup – and a friendly one!

# Cauliflower Soup

*Karfiolsuppe*

1 medium-size cauliflower
1 egg yolk
75ml (1/8 pint) milk or cream
1 3/4 litres (3 pints) water or stock

Salt, pepper, nutmeg
Chopped parsley
50g (2oz) butter
50g (2oz) flour

Cook cauliflower in salt water, being careful that it should not overcook. Lift out carefully, separate into small sprigs. Keep back a handful of sprigs, pass remainder through a sieve. Make a white roux with butter and flour, add water in which cauliflower has been cooked, cauliflower purée, salt, pepper and nutmeg. Simmer for a few minutes. Whisk egg yolk and milk, add hot soup gradually, return soup to stove, but do not boil. Add cauliflower sprigs, adjust seasoning and serve sprinkled with chopped parsley.

# Savoy Cabbage Soup

*Kohlminestrasuppe*

1³/4 litres (3 pints) stock
³/4–1kg (1¹/2lb) Savoy cabbage
150g (5oz) bacon
125g (4oz) rice

50g (2oz) Parmesan cheese
1 onion
Salt, pepper, marjoram

Cut bacon into cubes, melt over a low flame. Add chopped onion and fry until golden brown. Shred greens finely, scald with boiling water. Drain and add to onions together with stock. Salt, pepper and marjoram to taste. Add rice. Simmer until greens and rice are tender. Adjust seasoning. Serve with grated cheese.

Alternately, the shredded greens can be added to the fried onion (no scalding), remaining procedure as described above.

# Sour Cream Soup

*Stoss Suppe*

1 scant litre (1¹/2 pints) water
1 teaspoon caraway seeds
150ml (¹/4pint) sour milk
150ml (¹/4pint) sour cream

Salt
2 boiled potatoes cut
   into cubes
1 scant dessertspoon flour

Cook caraway seeds in water, with salt added, for 10 minutes. Slake flour with sour milk, add boiling water gradually, whisking all the time. Return to fire, bring to boil once, strain. Add sour cream carefully, heat, but do not boil. Serve with cooked, cubed potatoes – add a dash of vinegar or a few drops of lemon juice if necessary.

# *Austrian* cooking

# Tomato Soup

*Paradeis Suppe*

1kg (2lb) tomatoes
1 onion
2 carrots
Small piece celeriac
90g (3oz) butter
60g (2oz) flour

A little lemon juice
Sugar to taste
60g (2oz) cooked rice
Grated lemon rind
Bay leaf
Salt, pepper

Wash tomatoes, cut into halves. Scrape carrots, slice. Cut onion finely. Melt butter, fry onion until golden brown. Sprinkle with flour, fry lightly. Add halved tomatoes, carrots, chopped celeriac, bay leaf, grated lemon rind, salt and pepper. Cover with water or stock (about 1 1/2 litres (2 1/2 pints)), and simmer until vegetables are soft. Pass through sieve. Add sugar and lemon juice (do not be afraid of adding a generous amount of sugar – about three tablespoons – as tomato soup should have a distinctly sweet flavour). Place rice in centre of soup bowl, pour hot soup over it and serve.

# *Mushroom Soup*

*Schwammerlsuppe*

250g (1/2lb) mushrooms
60g (2oz) butter
30g (1oz) flour
1 1/2 litres (2 1/2 pints) water
1 small onion

1 tablespoon chopped parsley
Salt, pepper
A little lemon juice
75ml (1/8 pint) cream

Clean and slice mushrooms. Chop onion. Fry onion in butter until transparent, add sliced muchrooms, parsley, lemon juice, salt and pepper. Cover with a lid and simmer until mushrooms are soft, adding a little water if necessary. When mushrooms are cooked, dust with flour, stir and gradually add the water. Cook for another 20 minutes, stir in cream 5 minutes before serving, taking care that soup should not boil after cream has been added.

# *Austrian* cooking

## *Fish*

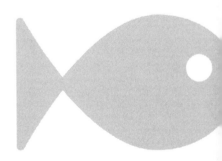

# Fish

Lakes and rivers in Austria yield a large variety of superb fish, the preparation of which is kept very simple. A respectable carp or trout is cooked *au bleu* – not really an Austrian recipe, but a way of cooking fish widely adopted throughout Austria. Or it is baked in the oven with lots of butter and possibly cream. In the case of larger fish, such as pike or carp, it is quite often sliced, floured, egged and breadcrumbed and then fried. Then there is also fish in aspic jelly with some regional variations.

Mention 'sea fish' to an Austrian housewife and watch her turn up her nose. In an emergency perhaps, and even then with reservations. The preliminaries alone would fill a book. Soak in milk. Wash in vinegar... the main reason being that Austria is really too far away from the sea so that when the fish arrives it is generally quite a bit past its first prime. All of which accounts for the absence of recipes concerning cod, haddock and the like, though most of the recipes given on the following pages are suitable for any type of white fish.

*Austrian* cooking

# Carp in Aspic

*Gesulzter Karpfen*

Wash, clean and scale a carp, cut it into pieces 2.5cm (1in) wide. Cut one onion, two carrots, one celeriac into strips and cook them in salt water until tender. Strain liquid into another saucepan, set aside the cooked vegetables. Make up the liquid to 1 1/8 litres (2 pints), add a few peppercorns, a bay leaf, salt, a little lemon juice, thyme and two tablespoons good wine vinegar and simmer for 20 minutes. Add the carp, including the head (having removed the gills, etc.) and simmer until the fish is cooked – about 12 to 15 minutes. Lift out the fish carefully and arrange it in a deep dish, leaving a little space between each slice, but arranging the slices graded so that the head is at one end and the tail at the other. Sprinkle the cooked vegetables round the fish and between the slices, adding a few chopped pickled cucumbers. Reduce stock in which the fish was cooked to half by cooking it briskly in an open pan, adjust the seasoning, adding a little more vinegar if necessary, then strain it over the fish. Leave to set.

My grandmother always cooked some potatoes in the stock which she would then slice and arrange round the fish, together with the other vegetables and sometimes she would also stir a handful of ground walnuts into the strained stock before pouring it over the fish.

# Eel with Parsley

*Gebratener Aal*

Wash and skin an eel, cut it into slices and sprinkle it with salt. Leave for 30 minutes. Wipe the eel with a clean cloth, arrange the slices in a frying pan, sprinkle with pepper and finely chopped parsley and add half a tumbler of white wine. Simmer over medium flame, turning the eel slices from time to time until thoroughly cooked and browned on top. No fat is needed, the eel will provide its own. If it appears to cook too quickly, clamp a lid over the frying pan for a few minutes.

# Pike in Cream Sauce

*Gespickter Hecht*

Wash, clean and scale a pike, make a few incisions down the back and stuff it with small slivers of anchovy. Sprinkle fish with a little pepper. Melt a piece of butter in a baking dish, turn over the fish in the melted butter so that it is well covered. Add a few broken-up tomatoes, a little lemon juice and 150ml (1/4 pint) sour cream or yoghurt. Bake the fish at 200°C/400°F/Gas 6, basting frequently. Sprinkle with breadcrumbs and return it to the oven for a few minutes to brown.

# Baked Pike

*Gebratener Hecht*

Wash, clean and scale a pike. Cream 100g (3oz) butter with three finely scraped anchovies and spread thickly over the fish. Sprinkle the fish with breadcrumbs and put it in a baking dish. Bake at 190°C/375°F/Gas 5, basting frequently. Peeled and sliced potatoes can be put around the fish and baked at the same time, but they must be dotted with butter before the dish is put in the oven.

# Carp in Paprika Sauce (Cold)

*Gesulzter Paprikakarpfen*

Wash, clean and scale a carp and cut it into slices. Take the weight of the fish in onions and slice them very finely. Barely cover the onions with water and cook until tender, add 2 dessertspoons paprika, salt and stir. Add the fish and simmer gently, without stirring, until the fish is tender. Lift out the fish and arrange it on a platter. Sieve the sauce and pour it over the fish. Put in a cold place to set.

# Pike with Anchovy Butter

*Hecht Mit Sardellenbutter*

Wash, clean and scale a pike. Make a few incisions down the back of the fish and stuff the slits with thin slivers of anchovy. Melt a lump of butter in a baking dish, add the pike and bake at 200°C/400°F/Gas 6, basting frequently. Set the fish on a serving dish and keep it warm. Pound four anchovies to a paste. Melt 75g (3oz) butter in a pan, add the pounded anchovies, stir and pour hot over the fish.

# Carp with Sour Cream

*Karpfen Mit Rahm*

Clean, wash and scale a carp, leaving it whole. Make several incisions down the back of the fish, sprinkle with salt and pepper. Butter a deep fireproof dish well, cover bottom with scraped and sliced new potatoes, dot with butter and sprinkle with salt and pepper. Pour about a 150ml (1/4 pint) of sour cream over it and place the fish on top. Pour another 150ml (1/4 pint) of sour cream over the fish, dot with butter. Bake at 180°C/350°F/Gas 4 for about 30 minutes, basting frequently, then increase the heat to 220°C/425°F/Gas 7, sprinkle with breadcrumbs, dot with a little more butter and return it to the oven to complete baking.

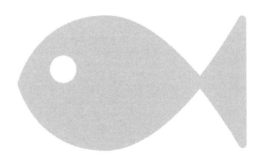

# *Fish in Marinade*

*Marinierte Bratfische*

Specially suitable for small fish such as herrings, etc. If larger fish is to be used, it must be cut into suitable pieces. Wash and clean fish, wipe dry. Sprinkle with salt, paprika and dust with flour. Brown quickly in hot oil on both sides and arrange the fish in a deep earthenware or heatproof glass dish. In the same oil fry a finely sliced onion and 1 or 2 sliced mushrooms. Sprinkle with chopped parsley and add two sliced tomatoes, stirring all the time. Now add 150ml (1/4 pint) of good wine vinegar and 300ml (1/2 pint) of water (or 450ml (3/4 pint) of white wine), one bay leaf, a sprig of thyme, one clove, salt and pepper and, if you like garlic, a crushed clove of garlic. Simmer for 10 minutes, then pour the marinade hot over the fish, which should be completely covered. Cover the dish with muslin and leave to stand for 2 or 3 days in a cold place. Serve sprinkled with chopped parsley.

# *Fish cooked in Brown Ale*

*Schwarzfisch*

Although this recipe was originally intended for carp and similar river fish, any white fish, including cod and haddock may be used.

Clean the fish, and cut it into convenient pieces. Sprinkle with salt. Clean and slice 1 celeriac, 1 lemon, including the rind, and one large onion. Put celeriac, lemon and onion in a saucepan, together with five lumps of sugar, five peppercorns, a blade of mace and a piece of root ginger. Cover with 425ml (3/4 pint) of water and 425ml (3/4 pint) of brown ale and bring to boil. Reduce heat and simmer for 20 minutes. Then add the fish and simmer until tender. Lift out the fish and keep it warm. Add about six tablespoons grated honeycake to the stock in which the fish was cooked, two tablespoons butter, two tablespoons dark plum jam or redcurrant jelly, one tablespoon each of raisins and sultanas, one tablespoon blanched almonds cut into strips and a few walnuts. Bring to boil and pour over the fish. Serve hot – and this is one of the dishes which taste better every time they are warmed up!

*Austrian* cooking

# *Meat, Game and Poultry*

# *Veal Ragout*

*Eingemachtes Kalbfleisch*

400g (3/4lb) veal
1 onion
2 carrots
1 celeriac or top part celery
Salt, pepper
125g (4oz) mushrooms
45g (1½oz) butter
30g (1oz) flour

Small knob butter
½ cup milk
1 egg yolk
125g (4oz) packet frozen peas
½ small cauliflower
A little lemon juice
Chopped parsley

Cut meat into convenient pieces. Put in a saucepan, together with carrots, onion, celery and cauliflower divided into small sprigs. Cover with water, salt and pepper to taste. Simmer very gently until meat is tender. Remove onion and celery. Melt butter, add sliced mushrooms, cover with a lid and simmer until mushrooms are cooked. Stir flour into melted butter, cook but do not brown. Gradually add stock from meat, stirring all the time. Add peas to meat and pour sauce over it. Slice carrot and return to meat. Simmer for another 10 minutes. Stir egg yolk into milk, add to meat, stirring all the time and taking care that mixture should not boil. Just before serving add a small knob of butter and a little lemon juice. Sprinkle with chopped parsley.

*Austrian* cooking

# Roast Knuckle of Veal

*Gebratene Kalbsstelze*

This is sold by weight in most restaurants. Sizes vary greatly and when your *Kalbsstelze* arrives, all nicely browned and glistening, it will usually bear a little label somewhere, proclaiming its weight. The best of them are larded before roasting, a little trouble well worth while.

2 knuckles veal
Strips bacon
Salt, pepper

1 tablespoon dripping
Water or stock

Lard knuckles of veal neatly, sprinkle with salt and a little pepper. Melt dripping in a baking dish, toss meat in melted dripping, cover with a lid and roast in oven, adding a little water from time to time (190°C/375°F/Gas 5). Remove lid towards end of roasting to brown meat. When the meat is tender and nicely browned, take it out of the tin and keep hot. Add a little water or stock to the juice in the baking dish, stir well and cook a little to reduce. Pour over meat and serve.

# Stuffed Breast of Veal

*Gefuellte Kalbsbrust*

1kg (2lb) breast of veal
2–3 rolls
Milk
1 egg
Parsley

1 small onion
Salt, pepper
125g (4oz) mushrooms
1 heaped tablespoon butter

Loosen rib bones, but do not remove them. Make an incision between meat and bones to form a pocket. Sprinkle meat with a little salt and pepper. Grate onion finely, clean and slice mushrooms. (Fewer mushrooms may be used or mushroom stalks only.) Melt butter in a frying pan, add grated onion and fry lightly. Throw in sliced mushrooms and chopped parsley and simmer until tender. Remove crust from rolls and soak them in a little milk, then squeeze out all the moisture and add rolls to mushrooms. Fry for about 30 seconds, mix well with a wooden spoon. Remove frying pan from heat, add the egg, chopped parsley and salt and pepper to taste. Fill the meat 'pocket' with the stuffing, sew up opening. Place meat in a roasting tin, add a lump of butter, cover with a lid and roast slowly (160°C/325°F/Gas 3). Add a little water or stock during the roasting and remove lid of roasting tin towards the end. Before serving take out the thread and slice meat downwards between the bones.

# Veal Goulash

*Kalbsgulasch*

500g (1lb) veal
250g (8 oz) onions
Fat for frying
Salt

1 tablespoon paprika
150ml (1/4 pint) sour cream
1 tablespoon tomato purée
1 tablespoon flour

Chop onions or cut them into rings. Fry onions in fat until golden brown, dust with paprika, stir, then add about two tablespoons water. Cut meat into cubes, dust with flour and add to onions. Fry lightly until water has evaporated. Add tomato purée, salt and cover with a lid. Simmer very gently until meat is tender, adding a little water as this becomes necessary. Finally stir in the sour cream, cook for a few more minutes and serve with *Nockerl* (page 90).

*Austrian* cooking

# Boned Knuckle of Veal

*Kalbsvoegerl*

There is more in a knuckle of veal than meets the eye. If you remove the bone (cutting right down to the bone first and shaving carefully all round it – I use a so-called 'map-knife' for this purpose, available at most good stationers) you will find that the meat falls into several oblong portions according to the fibres of the meat. Separate meat into these portions, lard them with strips of bacon and take your choice from several good ways of cooking them: you can roll up the meat (along the fibres, not across), tie it securely with cotton or thin string and simmer the meat gently with onions, tomatoes and a few small carrots. Or you can roast them in the oven with a little dripping (covered baking dish, please) and finish them off in a cream sauce. Or, most satisfying of all, you can spread any good stuffing over the meat, roll it up as before and roast or braise the meat according to your taste.

Incidentally, veal thus prepared is called *Voegerl* (little birds) because when rolled and tied it resembles a small bird trussed for roasting or braising.

# Wiener Schnitzel

*Wiener Schnitzel* is simple enough to prepare – if you have the meat, that is (and the meat in this case should be best fillet of veal). Everybody in Vienna will tell you that. Just a nice piece of veal dipped in egg and breadcrumbs and fried. *And* you should be able to slip a knife easily between the coating and the meat. *And* the coating should be golden brown – not dark brown. *And* any self-respecting *Schnitzel* should about cover your plate (after frying). *And* some wicked people smother it in gravy, for no reason at all. *And* others decorate it with slices of hard-boiled egg *and* an olive *and* bits of anchovy curled round, when all a *Wiener Schnitzel* really longs for is just a nice wedge of lemon – not a coyly crimped slice which is of no use to anyone… As you will see from the following recipe, *Wiener Schnitzel* is, after all, just a nice piece of veal dipped in egg and breadcrumbs and fried. Here's how:

Trim veal escallops neatly, make a few incisions all round the edges. Beat escallops well. Have ready three soup plates: one with flour, one with egg mixed with a little cold milk and a pinch of salt, and a third one with good breadcrumbs (not toasted crumbs). Dip escallops first into flour, shake off surplus, then into the beaten egg and finally into the breadcrumbs. Do not press down the crumbs, just shake off surplus. Do not keep escallops too long before frying. Fry escallops in deep smoking hot lard or oil. Do not fry too many escallops at the same time. Fry until golden brown on one side, turn carefully, fry other side. Drain escallops on crumpled kitchen paper and keep hot. That is all – you may even trim your *Wiener Schnitzel* with a little bit of pickled cucumber (the small, sharp kind) if you wish! Average weight of escallop (before coating with flour, etc.): about 120–125g (4oz).

# Naturschnitzel

Trim escallops, make a few incisions around the edge and beat escallops well. Rub lightly with salt and pepper – some cooks also dust one side with a little flour. Melt some butter (or pure lard or good dripping) in a frying pan. Fry escallops on both sides (if the escallops have been floured, fry the floured side first), lift out and keep hot. Carefully pour off surplus fat, but see that all the little brown bits stay in the pan. Stir in a little stock, then add a good knob of butter. As soon as the mixture begins to bubble, pour over meat and serve at once.

# Veal Escalopes in Cream Sauce

*Rahmschnitzel*

| | |
|---|---|
| 4 veal escallops | Chopped capers |
| A little flour | Salt, pepper |
| Butter for frying | 1 teaspoon French mustard |
| 1/2 cup cream | Paprika |
| 1/2 cup water | Lemon juice |

Trim escallops, then beat well to flatten. Rub lightly with salt, dust one side with flour. Fry escallops in butter, lift out carefully and keep hot. Pour a little water into frying pan, stir, then add chopped capers, pepper, paprika and French mustard. Bring to boil, then stir in cream and lemon juice. Adjust seasoning, add a little more water, if necessary, stir and pour over meat. Serve at once.

*Austrian* cooking

# *Pariser Schnitzel*

Trim veal escallops neatly, make a few incisions round the edges and beat well. Sprinkle them with a little salt and pepper, flour lightly, then dip into beaten egg to which about a tablespoon milk has been added. Fry escallops in smoking hot fat or oil until golden brown on both sides, drain well... and as our old cook would say, 'they are very popular with the gentlemen'...

# *Steak à la Esterhazy*

*Esterhazy Rostbraten*

Trim small beefsteaks neatly, flatten with a mallet or a rolling pin. Sprinkle steaks with salt, pepper and paprika and a light dusting of flour. Cover bottom of a thick saucepan first with strips of bacon, then with an onion and a large carrot cut into strips. Add a bay leaf, a pinch of thyme and marjoram, a quartered tomato, a small celeriac and half a green pepper (both cut into strips). Sprinkle with salt, pepper and a teaspoon sugar. Cover with a lid and simmer gently (without stirring) until vegetables are softened a little, then remove the lid and brown vegetables without stirring, but adding a little water from time to time. (The temptation to 'give a good stir' is very great at that point – this you must not do, but you can shake the pan very lightly.) When the vegetables are nicely browned, add the steaks and toss lightly with the vegetables. Cover with a lid, simmer very gently until both meat and vegetables are tender, adding a little water if necessary. Arrange steaks on a hot dish, add a little sour cream to vegetables, stir well and pour over meat, having previously removed the bay leaf.

There is another version of the same dish where onions and carrots, etc., are cooked separately and only added to the meat before serving, but the recipe quoted above gives better gravy and juicier meat.

# Boiled Beef

*Gekochtes Rindfleisch*

See page 6 for *Klare Rindsuppe*.

# Matrosenfleisch

Cut 250–450g (1/2–3/4lb) of lean beef into strips, flattening each strip with the knife after cutting. Chop one large onion and fry until golden brown in about 2 tablespoons fat. Throw in the meat, add a pinch of marjoram, salt, pepper and cover with a lid. Simmer gently for 5 minutes, then add one tablespoon flour, a dash of vinegar and stir.

Continue simmering until meat is soft – about 20 minutes in all.

# Paprika Beef

*Paprika Rostbraten*

4 slices beef (fillet)
225g (8oz) onions
2 tablespoons fat
1 tablespoon flour
1 tablespoon paprika

150ml (1/4 pint) sour cream
Salt, pepper
3/4kg (11/2lb) potatoes
1 tablespoon tomato purée

Trim beef, beat well and rub with salt and pepper. Melt fat, fry meat lightly on both sides. Lift out meat and put in a fireproof dish or casserole. Chop onions and fry in fat until brown. Add paprika, flour and tomato purée, stir in 1 cup water. Pour over meat and cover with lid. Simmer gently either on top of stove or in oven, 160–180°C/325–350°F/Gas 3–4. Slice potatoes and add to meat about 45 minutes before serving. Stir in sour cream before serving, heat but do not let it boil. Adjust seasoning.

# *Beef Goulash*

## *Rindsgulasch*

*Gulyas* is a Hungarian national dish. *Gulasch* is an Austrian national dish. There the similarity ends. What is known in Austria as *Gulasch* the Hungarians refer to as *Pörkölt*. After that things get really complicated. In Austria you can take your choice from *Rindsgulasch* (goulash made with beef), *Kalbsgulasch* (goulash made with veal), *Debrecziner Gulasch*, *Znaimer Gulasch*, to quote but a few. The Hungarians say that there is no such thing as a *Gulyas* made with veal. Of course there is Pörkölt made with veal or *Paprikas* made with veal... And as for *Debrecziner Gulasch* (Debreczin is a town in Hungary), they have never even heard of it...

Anyhow, goulash is nice. All the year round. At all times of the day. In Vienna they talk lovingly of the good old days when a *Fruehstuecksgulasch* (breakfast goulash) only cost a few *Kreuzer*. (In case this debauchery shocks you, 'breakfast' in this case means 'elevenses'.)

You get the best goulash in a restaurant. 'Freshly made,' the waiter will assure you. 'How many days ago?' asks the prudent housewife, knowing full well that goulash tastes nicest when warmed up... And as for the vitamins that get destroyed that way... well, anybody in Vienna will assure you that there is nothing like a good *Gulasch* to give you strength!

| | |
|---|---|
| 3/4kg (1 1/2lb) beef | Fat for frying |
| 3/4kg (1 1/2lb) onions | Salt |
| 1 tablespoon paprika | Pinch marjoram, caraway seeds |
| 1 tablespoon tomato purée | Vinegar |
| (optional) | |

Slice onions finely, cut beef into cubes. Fry onions in fat until golden brown. Add paprika and stir once, then add two tablespoons water. Throw in the meat, keep stirring until water has evaporated. Add tomato purée, salt, a dash of vinegar, marjoram and caraway seeds and cover saucepan with a lid'. Simmer *very gently* until meat is tender, adding water only in very small quantities as it becomes necessary. When the meat is soft, add a little more water, increase heat under saucepan, stir well and cook goulash for a few more minutes.

If you want more gravy, add one tablespoon flour slaked in a little water before final adding of water, stir and then proceed as described above, adding a bigger quantity of water.

There are of course a hundred and one ways that lead to a perfect goulash. A crushed clove of garlic may be added with the caraway seeds, etc., or a green or red pepper cut into strips. A friend of mine always adds a dash of strong black coffee, another one insists on a tablespoon of vinegar, and I remember being told once that a teaspoon of grated lemon rind really makes all the difference...

Serve with *Nockerl* (see page 90), or bread dumplings (see page 91), or with plain boiled potatoes (add a pinch of caraway seeds to the water while cooking).

# *Marinaded Beef*

### *Sauerbraten*

| | |
|---|---|
| Small joint beef | 1 teaspoon sugar |
| 150ml (1/4 pint) red wine vinegar | 1 carrot |
| 150ml (1/4 pint) water | Sour cream, about 150ml (1/4 pint) |
| 1 bay leaf | Salt, pepper |
| 2 cloves | 1 tablespoon lard or dripping |
| Thyme | 2 onions |

Cut one onion into small pieces, put it in a saucepan with the vinegar and the water, bay leaf, cloves and thyme. Bring to boil and cook for 15 to 20 minutes, remove from heat and cool. Put meat in an earthenware bowl, pour over the cold marinade, taking care that meat should be completely covered. Cover bowl with a cloth. Leave meat in marinade for at least four days, longer if possible, turning it over from time to time. When required, take out the meat, fry with chopped onion, carrot and a little sugar. Add the strained marinade very gradually, as beef simmers in a covered casserole. Just before serving stir in sour cream, salt and pepper to taste.

*Austrian* cooking

# Wiener Rostbraten

Cut some beef steaks to the thickness of a finger. Trim off all fat, beat well. Make a few incisions round the edges. Sprinkle with a little lemon juice, rub with salt, pepper and some paprika. Melt a tablespoon of good lard in a frying pan, throw in the steaks and fry quickly on both sides. Lower heat and add about two tablespoons of chopped onion. Continue frying at lower heat, lift out steaks as soon as they are cooked. (This is important as they will harden if left too long.) Keep steaks hot. Fry onions to a nice golden brown. Pour off surplus fat add about one tablespoon butter, stir well and gradually add 3/4 cup stock. Bring to boil, adjust seasoning and pour quickly over steaks. Serve at once.

# Pot Roast Beef Stuffed with Frankfurters

*Wuerstelbraten*

I feel I ought to say here and now that this is, and always has been, my favourite way of cooking beef. That it is also an excellent way of making a small joint go almost twice as far is merely coincidental...

Take a lean joint of beef and trim off all fat. With the help of a skewer make 4 or 5 holes right through the joint, along the fibres of the meat. Push some Frankfurter sausages through the holes. If the sausages are longer than the joint, chop off at ends so that they do not protrude from joint. Fry one large chopped onion in a tablespoon fat, dust meat with salt, pepper and paprika and toss in hot fat with onion. Sprinkle with one tablespoon flour and fry for another minute. Transfer everything to an ovenproof dish, swill out frying pan with 1 cup water and pour over meat. Cover with a lid and cook gently in oven until meat is tender (160°C/325°F/Gas 3). Add a little more hot water during cooking if necessary. Pass gravy through a sieve before serving (it may be thickened with some sour cream, but this is purely optional). Serve meat sliced (across sausages, so that each slice has some small rounds of sausage in it) with the gravy poured over.

# *Bruckfleisch*

*Bruckfleisch* is the name for a collection of beef offal, consisting of sweetbreads, liver, heart, melts plus a piece of *Kronfleisch* which is a cheap cut of beef.

500g (1lb) Bruckfleisch
  (see above)
Small piece of celeriac
  or celery
2 carrots
1 onion
Parsley, including roots

2 tablespoons vinegar
2 tablespoons fat
Pinch marjoram, thyme,
  caraway seeds
1 bay leaf
Salt, pepper
1 tablespoon breadcrumbs

Grate carrot, celeriac and onion. Chop parsley. Cut meat and offal into smallish pieces. Fry vegetables light golden brown in fat, add meat, etc., and toss in hot fat for a few minutes. Add breadcrumbs, stir, then add vinegar and a little water. Add bay leaf, thyme, marjoram, caraway seeds, salt and pepper. Cover with a lid and simmer gently until all the meat is soft. Remove bay leaf, adjust seasoning and serve with dumplings.

# **Roast Pork with Cream Sauce**

*Jungfernbraten Mit Rahmsauce*

Lard a lean piece of pork (suitable for roasting) with strips of bacon. Rub the meat with salt, pepper, paprika and sprinkle with caraway seeds. Cut a medium onion into rings and chop a few sticks of celery into small pieces. Also chop a little parsley, some parsley root and 1 or 2 carrots. Melt a tablespoon of dripping or lard in a frying pan, throw in the vegetables and brown them lightly. Transfer vegetables to a roasting tin, add the meat and very little water. Cover tin with a lid and cook meat slowly in oven (150°C/300°F/Gas 2), adding more water during the cooking. Remove lid of tin when meat is almost cooked. Take the meat out of the roasting tin, slice meat and keep hot. Add a small tub or jar of sour cream to vegetables, etc., in tin, stir well and strain over meat. The gravy may be thickened with a little flour, but this is generally not necessary. Garnish meat with capers and chopped parsley.

*Austrian* cooking

# Pork with Horseradish

*Krenfleisch*

Usually this consists of part of a pig's head, one or two pig's trotters and a piece of pork belly. Chop meat into convenient pieces and place in a large saucepan. Add two onions, two carrots, a piece of celery, a few peppercorns, salt and a cupful of vinegar. Barely cover with water and simmer gently until meat is tender. Take out the meat and place it in a warmed soup bowl. Slice the carrots and add to meat. Reduce stock by cooking it uncovered for another 5 minutes. Strain some of the stock over meat and carrots, sprinkle thickly with grated horseradish. Serve with plain boiled potatoes.

# Roast Pork

*Schweinsbraten*

Rub meat with salt, pepper, French mustard and a crushed clove of garlic. Sprinkle with caraway seeds. Place meat in a baking dish, cover with a lid and roast in the oven 190°C/375°F/Gas 5. Baste frequently (a little water or stock may have to be added). When the meat shows signs of getting tender, remove lid of baking dish, make a few incisions in the fat right down to the meat and finish roasting without the lid. Place meat on a hot platter, pour off surplus fat from baking tin. Pour a little water or stock into baking tin, stir well and bring to boil. Cook for a few moments, serve gravy separately.

# Pork with Sauerkraut

*Krautfleisch*

350g (3/4lb) pork
225g (1/2lb) sauerkraut
Salt, pepper, paprika
Caraway seeds

1 clove garlic
1 small onion
1 dessertspoon fat

Crush garlic under the blade of a knife with a little salt. Cut onion into rings. Fry onion rings in melted fat until light golden brown, add salt, pepper and paprika and stir. Throw in the sauerkraut, the meat, previously cut into convenient pieces, and a little water. Add the garlic and the caraway seeds. Simmer very gently until meat is cooked, adjust seasoning and serve with potatoes or dumplings.

# Styrian Mutton Stew

*Steirisches Schoepsernes*

500g (1lb) mutton (weighed after
  all bones have been removed)
1 carrot
Fresh parsley and parsley root
1 small celeriac
1 onion

1 dessertspoon fat
Salt, peppercorns
Bay leaf, thyme
2 tablespoons vinegar
250g (1/2lb) potatoes

Cut meat into convenient pieces, pour some boiling water over it and leave for 10 minutes. Chop all the vegetables and fry lightly in fat. Pour away all surplus fat, add a scant litre (1½ pints) of water and bring to boil. Add meat, salt, peppercorns, bay leaf, thyme and vinegar. Simmer until meat is almost cooked, then add quartered potatoes and continue cooking until potatoes and meat are cooked.

   Arrange meat and potatoes in a deep bowl and strain soup over them. Often served with a little horseradish grated over the top.

# *Austrian* cooking

## *Lights*

*Beuschel*

Use veal lights for preference.

3/4kg (1 1/2lb) lights
1 onion
2 carrots
2 tablespoons vinegar
1 bay leaf
1 clove
A few peppercorns, salt
Parsley, celery
60g (2oz) fat

100g (3oz) flour
1 lemon
Sugar
Sour cream
A little French mustard
1 tablespoon chopped
  capers (optional)
2 anchovies (optional)

Wash lights well, place in a saucepan with onion, carrots, bay leaf, clove, peppercorns, salt, parsley, celery, a little grated lemon rind and vinegar and cover with water. Simmer until lights are cooked. Melt fat, stir in flour and prepare a brown roux. Add enough of the stock to make a thick sauce. Stir in finely chopped capers and anchovies, mustard, a pinch of sugar and a little lemon juice. Add lights cut into thin strips and just before serving stir in some sour cream. Serve with dumplings.

## *Brains in Egg and Breadcrumbs*

*Gebackenes Hirn*

Use calf's brains for preference. Bring some water to which salt and a little vinegar have been added to the boil. Add the brains and poach for a few minutes. Drain and remove skins from brains.

Leave brains to cool and then slice them. Dip brains first into flour, then into egg to which salt and pepper have been added and finally into breadcrumbs. Fry in smoking hot fat or oil. Serve with salad or vegetables.

# Fried Calf's Head

*Gebackener Kalbskopf*

1 calf's head
1/2 onion
2 peppercorns
Salt
2 carrots
Fresh parsley
Celery

1/2 lemon
1 egg
Flour
Breadcrumbs
Pepper
Fat or oil for frying

Pour boiling water over calf's head, leave to stand for 5 minutes, rinse with cold water. Place calf's head in a large saucepan, together with onion, carrots, parsley, celery, half a lemon, two peppercorns and the salt. Cover with water and simmer very slowly until meat is soft. Lift out the calf's head and leave to cool. (The stock in which it was cooked can be used for soup or aspic.) Remove bones from flesh (this should be very easy and bones should come away without any effort). Cut meat into convenient pieces if necessary. Dip meat first into flour, then into seasoned egg and finally into breadcrumbs. Fry in smoking hot fat or oil. Serve with salad and sauce tartare.

# Fried Calf's Liver

*Gebackene Kalbsleber*

250g (1/2lb) calf's liver
Flour
1 egg
Salt

Milk
Breadcrumbs
Fat or oil for frying

Cut liver into slices and soak them in milk for about 1 hour. Dry carefully in a cloth. Dredge liver with flour, dip into lightly beaten and salted egg and finally into breadcrumbs. Shake off surplus crumbs. Fry liver in smoking hot fat or oil, drain and serve with fresh green salad.

# Kidneys with Onions

*Geroestete Nieren*

Core and slice kidneys. Melt a large tablespoon good dripping in a frying pan and brown a finely chopped onion in this. Throw in the kidneys and fry, stirring constantly. When kidneys are nicely browned, add one teaspoon flour, stir and sprinkle with salt, pepper and a few caraway seeds. Gradually add about half a cup of water and a dessertspoon vinegar. Stir well and serve at once. Liver can be prepared in the same way.

# Roulade Filled with Calves Brains

*Hirnroulade*

250g (1/2lb) calf's brain
3 eggs
75g (2 1/2oz) cooked potatoes
  (passed through a sieve)
75ml (1/8 pint) top milk

30g (1oz) flour
1 small onion
Parsley
Salt, pepper
1 dessertspoon butter

Wash brains well and remove skin. Melt butter and add the brains. Fry brains very gently (cover frying pan if necessary) together with the chopped onion. Remove pan from heat, add salt, pepper and parsley, finally stir in one egg. Separate yolks and whites of two eggs. Beat yolks lightly, add potatoes and cream well. Gradually add the milk. Whisk egg whites with a pinch of salt until stiff, fold beaten egg whites into yolks and potatoes. Fold in the flour. Line a Swiss roll tin with buttered paper, sprinkle with a little flour. Spread mixture over this and bake in the oven at 190°C/375°F/Gas 5 for about 15 minutes. Remove paper at once, spread with brain filling and roll up as for Swiss roll. Return roll to oven for about 5 minutes (180°C/350°F/Gas 4). Slice roll and serve with green salad or vegetables.

# *Roast Mince*

*Faschierter Braten*

250g (1/2lb) beef
250g (1/2lb) pork
1 small onion
1 egg
2 day-old rolls

Salt, pepper
Parsley
Fat
Flour
Sour cream

Remove crust from rolls and soak in milk or water. Mince meat finely. Squeeze out moisture from rolls and add to meat, together with salt, pepper, egg, chopped parsley and finely chopped onion previously fried in a little fat. Knead well and shape into a roll. Dust with flour. If possible lay strips of streaky bacon on top. Melt a little fat or dripping in a baking dish, add the meat loaf, brush some of the melted fat over the meat, cover with a lid and roast in oven, removing bacon and lid towards the end to brown meat. Arrange meat on a heated dish, pour off surplus fat from baking dish and sprinkle in about one tablespoon flour. Stir well, gradually add enough water or stock to make a thick sauce and cook over low heat. Stir in a little sour cream and serve sauce separately. A few chopped capers may be added to the sauce.

*Austrian* cooking

# Tyrolean Liver

*Tiroler Leber*

500g (1lb) liver (calf's liver
  for preference)
Salt, pepper
50g (2oz) fat
Flour

1 small onion
75ml (1/8 pint) sour cream
1 tablespoon capers
1 tablespoon vinegar

Slice liver and dust lightly with flour. Melt fat and fry the liver. Take out liver and keep it hot. Fry chopped onion in the same fat, dust with a tablespoon flour and stir. Add salt, pepper, chopped capers, vinegar and sufficient water to make a thick sauce. Gradually add the sour cream. Heat, but do not boil. Return liver to sauce, serve after 3 to 4 minutes. Rice is a good accompaniment, so are dumplings or *Nockerl* (page 90).

# Potato Goulash

*Erdaepfelgulasch*

1kg (2lb) potatoes
2 onions
1 teaspoon caraway seeds
Pinch marjoram

Salt, pepper, paprika
2 pairs Frankfurter sausages
1 tablespoon dripping
1 rasher bacon

Peel and slice potatoes (about the thickness of a pencil). Chop onions. Cut bacon into small squares. Melt fat, add bacon and fry lightly. Add onions and brown. Throw in potatoes, add salt, pepper, paprika and caraway seeds. Stir, then add just enough water (or stock) to cover, and the sausage cut into cubes or slices. Simmer gently until potatoes are cooked. A tablespoon or two of sour cream can be added just before serving.

# Stuffed Green Peppers

*Gefuellte Paprika*

4 large green peppers
250g (1/2lb) lean mince (preferably
  beef and pork mixed)
60g (2oz) rice

1 dessertspoon fat
1 small onion
Chopped parsley
Salt, pepper

## Tomato Sauce

500g (1lb) tomatoes
1 tablespoon flour
Salt, pepper

1 small onion
1 tablespoon fat
A little lemon juice
Sugar

Slice or quarter tomatoes, chop onion. Melt the fat in a thick saucepan, add onions and brown lightly. Throw in the tomatoes, salt, pepper and a little sugar to taste. Fry for a few minutes, then add the flour and stir. Cover with water, add a little lemon juice and simmer until tomatoes are pulpy.

Cut tops off peppers, remove inside parts and pour hot water over peppers. Leave for 5 minutes, drain off the water. Melt the fat, fry chopped onion lightly in the fat, add rice and fry until rice is transparent. Add 3/4 cup water and simmer until water has been absorbed. The rice should then be half-cooked. Add the mince, parsley, salt and pepper. Mix everything together and fill peppers. Replace pepper tops and stand the peppers in a deep casserole.

Pass the tomatoes, etc., through a sieve. Mix together tomato purée and liquid and pour over peppers in casserole. (The tomato sauce should be fairly thin.) Cover casserole with a lid and either bake in oven (160°C/325°F/Gas 3) or cook on top of stove over a very low heat until meat and peppers are cooked. Serve with rice or plain boiled potatoes.

# *Austrian* cooking

## G'roestl *(sometimes known as Tiroler G'roestl)*

2 tablespoons good dripping
1 large onion
2 cups cooked beef,
  sliced

2 cups cooked potatoes,
  sliced or cubed
Salt, pepper and caraway seeds
Chopped parsley

Cut onion into rings. Melt half of the dripping in a frying pan, throw in onion rings and fry until golden brown. Lift out and keep hot. Add remaining fat, melt and throw in potatoes. Brown, then add meat. When meat and potatoes are nicely browned and crisp, return onions to frying pan, stir well, add salt, pepper and caraway seeds. Serve sprinkled with chopped parsley.

    There is a very similar Swedish dish, called *Pytt i panna*, which is, however, usually topped with a fried egg per portion.

# Saddle of Hare in Cream Sauce

### Hasenbraten mit Rahmsauce

1 saddle of hare
1 cup red wine
Sour cream
4 peppercorns
2 bay leaves
A little flour
Salt
Strips bacon for larding

1 onion
1 carrot
Fat for frying
Root ginger, thyme and marjoram
1 tablespoon cranberry or
  redcurrant jelly
1 clove garlic

Skin, trim and lard saddle of hare. Slice onions and carrots, put in a saucepan with peppercorns, bay leaves, thyme, root ginger, a clove of crushed garlic and marjoram. Cover with half a cup of water and simmer gently for 5 minutes. Add wine, heat, then remove from stove, pour over hare and leave for half a day. Take out hare, dry with kitchen paper. Melt fat in a baking dish, add hare, cover with a lid and roast in oven (190°C/375°F/Gas 5), adding marinade by the spoonful. When the meat is tender, slake sour cream with a teaspoon flour and add to sauce. Cook for another 10 minutes, then strain sauce over saddle of hare before serving, adding redcurrant jelly to sauce just before straining.

# *Leg and Loin of Venison in Cream Sauce*

*Rehbraten mit Rahmsauce*

Skin the meat, then lard neatly. Rub the meat with salt, pepper, crushed juniper berries and a little nutmeg. Slice an onion, two carrots and a celeriac. Melt a tablespoon fat in a saucepan, brown onion and other vegetables lightly in the fat. Add the meat, brown a little on both sides, then transfer meat and vegetables to a casserole. Add a teaspoon French mustard, a bay leaf, a little thyme, two cloves and a little grated lemon rind, also about 1 cup water or good stock. Cover casserole with a lid and simmer in oven (160–180°C/325–350°F/Gas 3–4) until meat is tender, adding a little more water during this time if necessary. Take out the meat, slice and keep hot on a platter. Add 150ml (1/4 pint) of red wine to the vegetables in the casserole, stir well, then add 150ml (1/4 pint) sour cream. Mix well together, heat and strain over the meat. Capers may also be added to the sauce. Serve with buttered noodles, or rice, and cranberries.

# *Fried Spring Chicken*

*Backhendl*

Clean and quarter poussins. Twist back the wings, make an incision on top of leg, twist back the legs. Dip chicken pieces first in flour, then in seasoned and lightly beaten egg, finally in breadcrumbs. Do not press down the crumbs, but shake off surplus. Clean chicken livers and stomach, also dip in flour, egg and breadcrumbs. Fry in smoking hot fat or oil until golden brown on both sides. Drain on crumpled kitchen paper and keep hot until all the chicken pieces have been fried. Serve with salad.

# Paprika Chicken

*Paprikahendl*

This is prepared in exactly the same way as Beef Goulash, using quartered chicken instead of the beef (see page 40). The chicken should be roasting chicken which is not quite as extravagant as it sounds (after all, simmering meat in gravy is always more economical than roasting it), but you can use a boiling fowl treated in the following way:

Clean but do not truss a boiling fowl. Put in a large saucepan together with an onion, two carrots, some celery tops, a little parsley, salt, pepper and the chicken giblets. Cover with water and simmer very gently for about 1 to 1 1/2 hours, depending on size of chicken. After that time take out the chicken and cut into convenient portions (as a boiling fowl is usually much bigger than a roasting chicken you can get 6 to 8 good portions that way). Melt a little fat in a saucepan and fry a large chopped onion until golden brown. Add a tablespoon paprika, stir once or twice, then pour in half a cup water. Add the chicken, sprinkle with salt and pepper and stir well until chicken is nicely browned. Add a teaspoon of caraway seeds (optional) and a little of the stock in which chicken was cooked. Cover with a lid and simmer very gently, adding more stock from time to time as it becomes necessary. When chicken is tender, add a little more stock, increase heat under saucepan, stir well and cook for another few minutes. If more gravy is wanted you can thicken it with flour and add accordingly more stock.

The remaining stock in which the chicken was pre-cooked makes excellent soup and you can, of course, use only half the chicken for Paprika Chicken, cooking the other half in the soup or serving it in a number of other ways.

# Ham Roll

*Schinkencremeroulade*

100g (4oz) cooked sieved potatoes
3 eggs
Pinch salt

1/8 litre (1/4 pint) milk (scant)
60g (2oz) flour
1 tablespoon chopped parsley

## Filling

50g (2oz) butter
100g (4oz) ham
2 anchovies

French mustard
Small gherkins

Separate egg yolks and whites. Beat together mashed potatoes and egg
yolks. Add milk, a pinch of salt and chopped parsley. Beat very well. Fold in
the stiffly beaten egg whites alternately with the flour. Spread mixture on a
baking sheet lined with buttered paper. (Do not worry if the mixture seems
too liquid, it stiffens considerably with the baking.) Bake at
190°C/375°F/Gas 5 until golden brown. Remove paper while still hot, roll
carefully over kitchen paper sprinkled with flour and leave to cool.

Prepare the filling thus: Cream butter, add the finely chopped ham and
the anchovies pounded to a paste. Beat in a little French mustard and some
chopped gherkins. Instead of the pounded anchovies a little tomato purée
may be used. Spread filling thickly over the cooled pastry, roll up again and
cut into thick slices. Serve with a salad, or with vegetables.

*Austrian* cooking

# Some Cold Dishes

# Aspic Jelly

*Aspik*

This forms a very essential part of the Austrian cuisine. The basic recipe quoted below can be varied according to supplies obtainable and alternate ingredients are given in brackets.

Into a large saucepan put one pig's trotter (or calf's foot), and a knuckle of veal (or one-quarter calf's head), all chopped into convenient pieces. If you have a chicken carcass, add this as well (or some of the giblets) and some ham and/or bacon rinds. Also add an onion, two large carrots, a celeriac (or some celery), parsley including some parsley root, 1 or 2 cloves, a few peppercorns, salt, a sliver of lemon peel, a bay leaf or two and some thyme. Personally, I also like to add a tomato broken in half and a few strips of green pepper. Add about 2–2¼ litres (4 pints) of water and 1 glass white wine (or half that of good wine vinegar). Bring to boil, do not skim, but lower the heat and simmer gently for 4 to 5 hours, until the meat literally falls from the bone. Strain the liquid into a bowl and leave to set. When the jelly has set remove all fat – this must be done very thoroughly. Put the jelly in a saucepan and heat. In a bowl whisk together one egg white (turkey or goose eggs are excellent for this as they are so much larger than chicken eggs), the juice of a lemon, a small glass of white wine (or good wine vinegar) and a little of the melted, but not yet hot jelly. Also add the crushed eggshells and mix everything well with an eggwhisk (this sounds far more complicated than it really is). Bring remaining jelly to boil and stir in the eggwhite mixture very carefully. Bring to boil again without stirring, then lower the heat immediately. Cover saucepan with a lid and leave liquid over the lowest possible heat for 15 minutes without any stirring. All the impurities will sink to the bottom. Strain the jelly through a clean cloth previously wrung out in cold water, taking great care not to stir up the sediment. If necessary, strain again through the cloth.

# Some Cold Dishes

## Aspic Jelly as Garnish

Prepare aspic jelly as described above, and pour into wetted, shallow moulds to set. Turn out on to greaseproof paper and cut into cubes. Treated this way, aspic jelly is often used to surround cold meat, sometimes sprinkled with a little Marsala or Madeira. Alternately, the aspic jelly is chopped rather fine and piped over cold meats, etc., through a forcing bag.

## To Line a Mould with Aspic Jelly

Melt the aspic over a low heat, remove as soon as it has melted and stir until cold. The aspic jelly must be quite smooth. Rinse the mould in cold water and pour in the aspic jelly. Chill it well in a refrigerator, until sides of mould are covered with a thin layer of aspic. Carefully pour the still liquid aspic jelly back into the saucepan. Now you can decorate the mould with anything you may fancy – small rounds of gherkins, hard-boiled eggs, etc., dipping each piece into the liquid aspic jelly and standing your mould either on a bed of crushed ice or in a bowl filled with iced water. Chill mould again so that the decorations can set into the lining, then fill the mould as required.

# *Austrian* cooking

## *Stuffed Chicken*

*Gefuelltes Huhn*

Clean a medium-sized roasting chicken. If you have it cleaned by the butcher, do remember to tell him not to truss the chicken for you, otherwise you will have holes in the skin, which is fatal. Cut the skin right down the back of the chicken, take off all the skin, being very careful not to tear it, and put it aside. Remove all the flesh from the bones (the carcass can be used for stock). Cut the white meat from the chicken breast into cubes, sprinkle with lemon juice and set aside. Weigh the remaining meat and add two-thirds of its weight in veal. Mince all the meat very finely, mince again or pass through a sieve. To the minced meat add salt, pepper, paprika, one tablespoon brandy, a few chopped black olives and two eggs. Work everything together until well blended, stir in 50g (2oz) of finely chopped bacon. Fold in the cubed white meat and, if possible, some cooked tongue, also cut into cubes. Stuff the chicken skin with this and, if you can, put 1 or 2 lightly fried chicken livers down the centre of the filling. Stuff chickern so that it almost takes back its previous form, sew up all the openings. Put the chicken in a roasting tin with a good lump of butter and brush it over with melted butter. Roast in a covered tin (190°C/375°F/Gas 5), removing cover towards the end so that the chicken browns nicely. Leave to cool in the baking dish, cover with a board and weigh down a little. Brush with liquid aspic jelly and leave to set before serving. Serve sliced downwards – or whole, surrounded with tomatoes stuffed with vegetable mayonnaise – but on no account attempt to carve it! It must be sliced downwards.

# *Brawn*

*Haussulz*

Into a large saucepan put a pig's trotter or a calf's foot, and half a calf's or pig's head, all chopped into convenient pieces. (Take out the brains beforehand and use separately.) Cover with about 2–2¼ litres (4 pints) of water, add a large onion, two carrots, two cloves, peppercorns, salt, some parsley including some root, a celeriac or a few pieces of celery, two bay leaves and ½ cup of vinegar. Bring to boil, then simmer very slowly for about 2½ to 3 hours until the meat is quite soft. Strain liquid into a bowl and leave to cool. Take all the meat from the bones and chop very fine. In Austria it is usual to add some smoked tongue or pork, cut into small pieces, but failing that a little boiled gammon, cut into cubes, will do very nicely. Remove all fat from the cooled liquid, add liquid to meat and heat. Bring to boil once, then remove it from the heat. Leave to cool a little, stirring so as to keep it well mixed. When cool, add some chopped gherkins, capers and quartered or sliced hard-boiled eggs. Taste the liquid when cold, add more seasoning and a little more vinegar – it should be quite sharp. Pour into a wetted mould and leave to set in a cold place. Turn out and serve cut into slices, sprinkled with finely chopped onion and a dressing of oil and vinegar.

If you possess a *Guglhupf* mould set the brawn in this – it looks rather nice. If you want to make a special effort, line the mould first with aspic jelly (see page 56–7) and decorate with slices of hard-boiled egg and cucumber.

# *Austrian* cooking

# *Galantine of Chicken*

*Huehnergalantine*

Clean a medium-sized roasting chicken, make a small incision on top of each leg, push back the skin and chop off the legs, leaving as much skin as possible. Treat wings in similar manner. Cut the chicken open down the back and bone it carefully, without tearing the skin. Put the chicken carcass in a large saucepan, together with the neck and stomach, a large onion, two carrots, peppercorns, salt, fresh parsley and, if possible, a small knuckle of veal or a calf's foot. Cover with about 2 litres (3½ pints) of water and simmer gently for 3 hours. Meanwhile, spread out the boned chicken and beat lightly with a mallet. Rub the meat with salt, pepper and a tiny pinch of nutmeg and sprinkle it with lemon juice. Remove all meat from the chicken legs and the wings and mince finely. Also mince about 250g (½lb) of lean veal. Mix together the meat and mince again or pass through a sieve. Fry 1 or 2 chicken livers lightly in a little butter, set aside. Swill out the frying pan with one tablespoon water and add it to the minced meat. Add two eggwhites and beat until smooth and quite firm. Beat in salt, pepper, paprika and about ½ cup cream. Fold in 60g (2oz) bacon cut into cubes, 125g (4oz) diced cooked tongue or gammon, a few chopped black olives and some chopped pistachios. Spread half of the filling over the chicken, place the chicken livers down the centre. Cover with remaining filling. Fold together chicken and sew up all openings. (Do not try to coax it back into its original shape – it should simply be oblong.) Tie chicken into a clean napkin, secure ends well and put it into the strained, hot chicken stock. Bring stock to boil, lower heat and simmer for about 45 minutes from then onwards. Take chicken out of the stock, remove napkin and leave chicken and stock to cool a little. Tie chicken into another napkin and put back into cooled stock, weigh down a little and leave overnight. Take out the thread, brush over chicken with liquid aspic jelly and leave to set. Serve sliced downwards.

# *Pâté of Chicken Livers*

*Huehnerleberpastete*

The original recipe calls for goose liver which is almost impossible to buy in this country – unless you buy the goose with it! Chicken livers are much easier to obtain and, of course, there are frozen chicken livers which are superb, if only one could get them more often.

Clean 500g (1lb) chicken livers, wash well. If using frozen chicken livers, four packets are about equivalent to 500g (1lb), taking into consideration weight lost through waste if using the fresh kind. Melt some butter in a saucepan (unless there is some fat clinging to the livers which could be rendered), add the livers and fry them very gently, covering the saucepan with a lid. This takes only a few minutes and care must be taken not to overcook the livers, as this will harden them. Set aside a few particularly nice pieces of liver, push the remaining livers through a sieve while still warm. Swill out the frying pan with one tablespoon brandy and one tablespoon Madeira or Marsala and pour over the sieved chicken livers. Cream two tablespoons butter, add the chicken livers, salt, pepper and nutmeg to taste. Beat in half a cup cream and about four tablespoons liquid aspic jelly. Cut the 'choice' pieces of liver into cubes and fold into the purée. Pile into a terrine, level top with a palette knife and cover with a thin layer of aspic jelly.

Alternately, you can line a mould with aspic jelly (see page 56–7), fill with the purée and put it in a cold place to set. Turn out and surround with cubes of aspic jelly.

*Austrian* cooking

# Katzenjammer

Correctly translated, this might be described as 'the morning after the night before'. It is a noted cure for hangovers of the milder type and, quite incidentally, an extremely pleasant dish for a light summer luncheon.

Cut some cooked beef into thin slivers or into cubes and cover with a marinade made of two parts oil, one part vinegar, salt, pepper and a little French mustard. Leave for 2 to 3 hours. Prepare the special mayonnaise described on page 79, seasoning it rather well. Lift the meat out of the marinade and fold into the mayonnaise. Also fold in some chopped gherkins and enough sliced potatoes to give a fairly loose consistency – on no account must the dish taste 'stodgy'. Sprinkle with paprika before serving.

# Ham Cornets

*Schinkenstanitzl*

Fry two chicken livers (or contents of half a packet of frozen chicken livers) lightly in butter. Do not let them overcook or they will harden – the whole process only takes about 3 to 4 minutes. Take out the livers and push them through a sieve. Swill out the frying pan with one tablespoon Madeira (or Marsala) and one tablespoon brandy. Pour liquid over sieved chicken livers. Mince 250g (½ lb) of ham finely, pass it through a sieve. Cream 125g (4oz) butter and beat in the chicken livers and the ham, salt, pepper, nutmeg and a little paprika to taste. Also beat in 2 to 3 tablespoons liquid aspic jelly (see page 56). Mix everything well and until quite smooth, then put it to set in a cold place. Trim some lean slices of ham into triangles. Put a tablespoon of the purée on each triangle and roll into a cornet. Arrange the cornets on a serving dish so that they rest on the folded part. Decorate the open end with a slice of hard-boiled egg and brush over the egg with liquid aspic jelly. Leave to set in a cold place.

# *Liptauer*

This is all a question of taste – except for the proportions of butter and cream cheese. Usually the amount of cream cheese is twice that of the butter. The butter is creamed and the cheese beaten in. After that you should add 1 or 2 finely scraped anchovies, some capers, gherkins and a small onion, all very finely chopped, also a pinch each of paprika, salt, pepper and caraway seeds and French mustard. You simply have to taste it (on a piece of bread) to see whether it suits your palate. Heap the cheese on to a large plate, decorate it with a few dents made with the back of a knife and sprinkle it with chopped chives – that is all. Or you can serve your *Liptauer* 'restaurant wise', that is to say, a small portion of cream cheese already mixed with butter in the centre of each plate, sometimes shaped like a large mushroom and dusted with paprika, surrounded by minute portions of all the ingredients that go into its making, and leave your guests to mix it to their liking.

*Austrian* cooking

## *Vegetables*

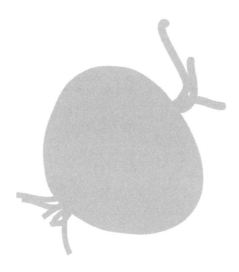

# *Vegetables*

When the Austrians feel virtuous about their vitamins, they cook their vegetables in what they fondly believe to be the 'English' way. They do not feel virtuous very often and even then they compromise by sprinkling a plainly boiled vegetable liberally with breadcrumbs fried to a crisp brown in best butter. This applies particularly to cauliflower, French beans and Brussels sprouts, which are usually served as a separate dish when prepared this way.

From the fair-sized range of typically Austrian vegetable dishes I have picked a few which are little known in this country. Some of these, like the methods for savoy and red cabbage, improve with each warming up. A dietitian's nightmare? I prefer to call it a good way to cook an otherwise rather dull vegetable.

# *Austrian* cooking

## *Brown Lentils*

*Braune Linsen*

Pick over 500g (1lb) brown lentils, wash them, then cover with cold water and leave to soak overnight. Pour away the water, put the lentils in a saucepan, together with an onion, a bay leaf, 1 or 2 carrots, a sliver of lemon peel, one tablespoon each of sugar and wine vinegar. A ham bone or even some bacon rinds tied together greatly improve the flavour. Cover with about a generous 3/4 litre (1 1/2 pints) water and simmer very slowly until lentils are tender. Dice about 90g (3oz) bacon, throw it into a frying pan and melt it down. Add a tablespoon flour, brown lightly and add it to the browned lentils. Simmer for another 10 minutes. Remove onion, bay leaf and ham bone. Slice carrots into the lentils. Adjust the seasoning, adding more vinegar and sugar. Together with bread dumplings (see page 91) this is the traditional accompaniment to smoked pork

## *Purée of Dried Yellow Peas*

*Erbsenpuree*

500g (1lb) dried yellow peas
Salt, pepper
Parsley

2 tablespoons butter
A few bacon rinds

Soak the peas overnight in cold water. Pour away the water, put the peas in a saucepan, together with a small bunch of parsley (including some parsley root if possible), some bacon rinds, salt and pepper, and water to cover. Cook until peas are quite soft. Drain, then pass peas through a sieve, adding a little of the water in which they were cooked, to obtain a stiff, but creamy consistency. Beat the butter into the hot purée and serve.

# Red or White Cabbage

*Geduenstetes Kraut*

1 red or white cabbage
  (weighing about 1½kg (3lb))
2 tablespoons sugar
3 tablespoons fat
2 tablespoons flour

Caraway seeds
Salt, pepper
Wine vinegar
Water or stock

Trim cabbage, cut off stalks, etc., and shred finely. Wash shredded cabbage well and sprinkle with salt. Fry the sugar in the fat until golden brown, quickly throw in the cabbage (stand away from the stove as it splutters a little). Toss the cabbage in the saucepan, add caraway seeds, pepper, two tablespoons vinegar and just enough stock or water to prevent burning. Simmer slowly, adding a little more water as it becomes necessary. Slake flour in ½ cup water and add towards the end of the cooking time (not less than about 10 minutes before serving). Adjust seasoning – it should have a distinctly sweet-sour flavour, adding more sugar or vinegar (or both). White wine can be used instead of water or stock and accordingly less vinegar. A grated apple is a good addition. Improves greatly with each warming up.

*Austrian* cooking

# French Beans in Cream Sauce

*Gruene Fisolen*

500g (1lb) French beans
1 small onion
1 heaped tablespoon chopped dill
1 heaped tablespoon butter

Juice 1/2 lemon
75ml (1/8 pint) sour cream
Salt, pepper, sugar

String the beans, wash and cut into 2.5cm (1in) pieces. Throw into 1 cup boiling salted water, cover with a lid and cook until tender. Chop onion and fry lightly in the butter together with the chopped dill. Sprinkle with flour and gradually add the water in which the beans were cooked together with a little more water or stock to make a thick sauce. Add sugar, salt and pepper to taste. Add the beans and lemon juice and adjust the seasoning. Just before serving stir in the sour cream. Heat but do not boil.

# Carrots

*Karotten*

500g (1lb) carrots
1 heaped tablespoon butter
1 tablespoon flour
1 small onion

Chopped parsley
Stock
Salt, pepper

Wash and scrape carrots, cut into slices. Chop the onion very finely and fry in the fat together with the sugar, until golden brown. Add the carrots, salt and pepper and cover with about 225ml (8fl oz) stock. Simmer until carrots are tender. Add some more stock, heat and stir in the flour slaked in 1/2 cup of water. Simmer for another 10 minutes, sprinkle with chopped parsley and serve.

## *Vegetables*

# *Carrots with Garden Peas*

*Karotten Mit Gruenen Erbsen*

Proceed exactly as for the previous recipe, cooking 125g (1/4 lb) of shelled peas with the carrots.

# *Potato Slices*

*Erdaepfelschnitten*

These are particularly good when served with game of any kind. Correctly they should be baked over a special mould so that they look like horseshoes, but the simpler shape does not alter the taste.

100g (3¹/2oz) cooked sieved potatoes
100g (3¹/2oz) butter
100g (3¹/2oz) flour
Salt

1 egg yolk
Grated Parmesan cheese,
  egg or milk for
  brushing over pastry

The sieved potatoes must be cold before work is commenced. Cut butter into small pieces, work to a smooth dough with the flour, salt, potatoes and the egg yolk. Cover with a cloth and leave for 20 minutes. Roll into a strip, fold sides to centre, fold over as for puff pastry. Cover and leave for 30 minutes. Roll out to 3mm (1/8in) thickness and cut into strips. Set the strips on a buttered and floured baking sheet, brush with egg or milk and sprinkle with grated Parmesan cheese. Bake at 200°C/400°F/Gas 6 until golden brown. Serve hot.

# *Austrian* cooking

## 'G'roeste'

Cook some small potatoes in their skins. Peel and leave to cool. Slice the potatoes or cut them into cubes. Melt about two tablespoons butter or good dripping in a thick frying pan, add the potatoes and fry them until nicely browned, stirring them from time to time to prevent burning, but not stirring often enough to reduce them to a pulp. Sprinkle with salt just before serving.

## Cos Lettuce with Green Peas

*Kochsalat mit gruenen Erbsen*

*1 large cos lettuce*
*500g (1lb) peas (before shelling)*
*1 small onion*
*Salt, pepper, sugar*

*1 tablespoon butter*
*1 tablespoon flour*
*Chopped parsley*
*About 1/8 litre (1/4 pint) milk*

Shell the peas, wash and shred the cos lettuce. Bring 1/2 cup of water to boil. Add salt, pepper and sugar and throw in lettuce and peas. Cook until tender. Drain, retaining the water. Melt the butter, add finely chopped onion and fry until pale brown. Stir in the flour and brown lightly. Add the water in which the vegetables were cooked and gradually stir in 150ml (1/4 pint) milk. Simmer for a few minutes, until flour is cooked. Add vegetables, stir well and serve.

# *Marrow*

Kuerbiskraut

Quarter a medium-sized marrow, remove seeds and peel. Shred the marrow, sprinkle with salt and leave to stand for 30 to 45 minutes. Melt two tablespoons butter, add half of a finely chopped small onion and brown lightly. Stir in two scant tablespoons flour, a little chopped parsley and dill, and a pinch of paprika. Stir in sufficient water or stock to make a thick sauce, simmer for a few minutes until well blended. Squeeze out all moisture from the marrow and add to the roux. Add a scant 140ml (1/4 pint) sour cream, a squeeze of lemon juice and a pinch of sugar. Cover with a lid and simmer for about 30 minutes.

# *Rice*

Reis

The following two ways of cooking rice are the ones mainly favoured in Austria:

## *First Method*

2 cups rice
3 cups good clear stock

1–2 tablespoons butter
Salt

Two tablespoons butter should really be used, one tablespoon only will do and there have been numerous occasions when I managed to get by with just a teaspoon of butter – but do not use margarine instead, it just doesn't work.

Wash the rice in hot water, dry in a sieve, shaking occasionally. Add butter to stock, salt to taste and bring to boil. Throw in the rice, let it boil up once, then lower the heat immediately. Simmer very gently in a covered saucepan until rice is tender.

*Austrian* cooking

## Second Method

2 cups rice
2 tablespoons butter or good
  dripping or oil

1 medium onion
Salt, pepper
4 cups water or stock

Wash the rice in hot water, drain well. Heat the fat in a thick saucepan, add rice and finely chopped onion and stir over a low heat until the rice looks transparent. Add boiling water or stock, salt and pepper to taste. Cover with a lid and simmer very gently until rice is tender, about 20 minutes. Remove saucepan lid, put a clean napkin over saucepan to absorb any remaining moisture.

    N.B. Using either method, the rice can be cooked in the oven instead of on top of the stove, 160–180°C/325–350°F/Gas 3–4.

# Risi Bisi

Fry 2 cups rice with a small, finely chopped onion in two tablespoons fat until rice looks transparent. Add 3 cups boiling water, salt and pepper, cover with a lid and simmer rice very slowly. Hold one packet of frozen peas under running cold tap to thaw, empty contents of packet into a bowl. When all the water has been absorbed by the rice, but rice is not quite tender, add the drained peas and simmer for another 5 minutes. Just before serving remove saucepan lid and place a clean napkin over the saucepan to absorb any remaining moisture.

# Savoy Cabbage Viennese Style

*Kohl*

1kg (2lb) savoy cabbage
1 small onion
125g (4oz) bacon or
  60g (2oz) butter
60g (2oz) flour
4 potatoes, parboiled

Parsley
Salt, pepper
1 clove garlic
Caraway seeds, marjoram
Stock

Wash, shred and cook cabbage in very little salt water. Cut bacon into cubes, melt them in a saucepan and fry the chopped onion in the fat. Add the chopped parsley, the flour and stir. Gradually add enough stock to make a thick sauce. Add the cooked savoy cabbage, the parboiled and cubed potatoes, salt, pepper and the clove of garlic crushed with salt under the blade of a knife. Simmer until potatoes are soft, adding a little more stock if necessary.

# Sauerkraut

Taste a bit of the Sauerkraut before cooking and also while it is cooking – it may be that the Sauerkraut is not quite sharp enough, in which case you will have to add a little vinegar.

For 500g (1lb) of Sauerkraut slice a small onion finely and brown it in about two tablespoons rendered bacon fat. Add the Sauerkraut, salt, one teaspoon caraway seeds and a little pepper. Cover with water or stock and a dash of white wine (optional) and simmer gently. After 30 minutes, grate two medium potatoes into the Sauerkraut and continue to simmer it for another 30 to 45 minutes. Adjust seasoning before serving.

# Mushroom Soufflé

*Schwammersoufflee*

250g (1/2lb) mushrooms
Salt, pepper
Butter for frying
4 eggs

50g (1 1/2oz) butter
30g (1oz) flour
1/4 litre (1/2 pint) milk

Heat oven to 200°C/400°F/Gas 6. Prepare soufflé dish (butter it well and tie a strip of buttered paper round it to come about 7.5cm (3in) over the top of the dish). Flour the soufflé dish lightly. Clean the mushrooms, slice them thinly. Fry mushrooms in butter, cover the frying pan with a lid and simmer the mushrooms until tender. Salt and pepper to taste.

Melt the butter, add flour and stir well. Gradually add the milk and cook mixture until it leaves sides of pan clean. Salt and pepper to taste. Remove from heat, stir until cooled a little. Beat in the egg yolks gradually, fold in stiffly beaten eggwhites and finally the mushrooms. Pour into prepared soufflé dish and bake until well risen and golden brown.

# *Salads*

# *Austrian* cooking

Salads are many and varied in Austria. There is lettuce salad (quartered lettuce tossed in dressing, quite often decorated with quartered hard-boiled eggs), lamb's lettuce (corn) salad, cauliflower salad made with cooked cauliflower broken into sprigs, lentil salad – with bits of chopped bacon or ham and chopped onion, beetroot salad – sliced beetroot with a little grated horseradish and a sprinkling of caraway seeds, tomato salad – with chopped onion, parsley and chives. Salads made with slices of cooked celeriac or lightly cooked French beans and a delicious salad of crisp green peppers cut into rings. And then of course there is potato salad with plenty of freshly ground black pepper and chopped onion. In each case the dressing is an ordinary French salad dressing of 2 or 3 parts oil to 1 part vinegar, with salt and pepper, a pinch of sugar and French mustard added, as the case may be. Theoretically...

In practice the proportions are quite often reversed and sometimes a little water is added to make the dressing less sharp. Or, probably, remembering the original proportions of 2 or 3 parts oil to 1 part vinegar, the oil is partly or wholly replaced by water and just a drop of oil is added, as an afterthought. All this results in a tendency to have too much dressing so that the salad – this applies particularly to lettuce salad – literally floats in it. Sometimes quite a bit more sugar than is strictly necessary is added, and if the vinegar is then replaced by lemon juice (which is quite often the case), the whole thing is rather like lemonade... Tackle someone about this aberration of taste and you will be given one of two answers: that a member of the household is on a strict diet, or that everybody likes it that way.

The situation is not utterly devoid of humour. Only quite recently an innocent visitor described one of these concoctions as 'wilted lettuce salad' – thinking that this was the effect intended!

The dressing may not be new to you, but perhaps you had never thought of making a salad with some of the vegetables quoted above and on the following pages. Incidentally, all vinegar used is wine vinegar – red or white and all oil is olive oil.

# Cabbage Salad *(Warm)*

*Warmer Krautsalat*

Remove stalks, etc., from a white cabbage. Wash well and shred the cabbage finely. Cover with boiling water and leave to stand for 30 minutes. Mix 1/8 litre (1/4 pint) good wine vinegar with the same amount water, add salt, a little sugar and a teaspoon caraway seeds, heat. Drain the water off the cabbage, pour the vinegar, etc., over it when boiling. Leave to stand for 15 minutes, drain off moisture, heat and pour again over cabbage. Repeat until all the dressing has been soaked up by the cabbage (partly it will of course have been reduced through the heating). Cut some bacon into cubes, put them in a saucepan and render down the fat. Pour hot over the salad – including the small crispy bits in the pan.

# Cucumber Salad

*Gurkensalat*

Slice a cucumber thinly. There is a cutter specially designed for this and similar jobs, called a 'Mandoline'. Sprinkle the sliced cucumber with salt, cover and leave for 30 minutes. Drain off all moisture by putting the cucumber in a clean cloth and squeezing lightly.

Rub a salad bowl with a cut clove of garlic, prepare a salad dressing consisting of three parts oil and one part vinegar, pepper, French mustard and a tiny pinch of sugar. Toss cucumber in the dressing, dust with paprika and sprinkle with chives.

*Austrian* cooking

# Cabbage Salad

*Krautsalat*

Remove stalks, etc., from a small red or white cabbage. Wash well and shred cabbage very finely. Sprinkle with salt and caraway seeds, put it in a bowl and pour boiling water over it. Cover bowl and leave for 30 minutes. Prepare a salad dressing with two parts oil, one part vinegar, pepper, sugar and a little French mustard. Drain off all moisture from the shredded cabbage, squeeze it lightly between the hands. Toss the shredded cabbage in the dressing.

# *Potato Mayonnaise*

*Mayonnaise Salat*

In Austria special potatoes called *Kipfler* ('shaped like a croissant') are used for this, and more often than not the mayonnaise is one prepared in the usual way – an egg yolk mixed with a teaspoon vinegar, a pinch of salt and pepper, to which about 150ml (1/4 pint) good oil is added drop by drop until the mayonnaise is thick. A little more vinegar (or lemon juice) is then stirred in, together with about one teaspoon French mustard and the sliced and still slightly warm potatoes (previously cooked in their skins and peeled) are folded in. So far I have never managed to buy *Kipfler* in England, but some of the potatoes which are imported from the Channel Islands are very similar. Actually any small waxy potato is quite suitable.

The special recipe for mayonnaise quoted below is particularly suitable for potato mayonnaise because it is fluffy rather than thick and to a certain extent soaks into the potatoes. It is equally good for a mayonnaise incorporating any other vegetable, fish, or meat, and in addition to this it is rather quickly prepared and uses only a tablespoon of oil.

*1 egg*
*1 egg yolk*
*4 tablespoons vinegar*
*2 tablespoons water*

*1 teaspoon French mustard*
*Salt, pepper*
*1/2 teaspoon sugar*
*1 tablespoon oil*

Place all ingredients, except the oil, in a bowl and whisk over steam until thick. Remove from heat, whisk in the oil, continue whisking until cooled. Fold in the sliced potatoes which should still be a little warm.

# *Mushroom Salad*

*Schwammerlsalat*

Clean and slice some mushrooms – field musrooms for preference – and throw them into boiling salt water. Cook for a few minutes only, drain well. Prepare an oil/vinegar dressing made of two parts oil and one part vinegar, salt and pepper to taste. Toss the mushrooms in this dressing while still hot, sprinkle a little finely chopped spring onion over the top before serving.

# Savoury Sauces

# Sauce Made with Dried Beans

*Bohnensauce*

This may sound rather unusual, but it is very good with boiled beef.

Soak about 1 cupful butter beans in cold water overnight. Pour away the water, put the beans in a saucepan, cover with water and cook until soft. Pass the beans through a sieve, then add two tablespoons oil, salt, pepper and vinegar or lemon juice to taste. Also add a small very finely chopped onion and/or some chopped chives. Blend very well and thin down a little with 1 or 2 tablespoons clear beef broth. Serve cold with boiled beef.

# Dill Sauce

*Dillensauce*

Chop one small onion finely and fry in one tablespoon butter until pale golden brown. Add one tablespoon each chopped parsley and chopped dill and stir. Sprinkle with one tablespoon flour, stir and gradually add 150ml (1/4 pint) of clear beef broth, the juice of half a lemon, salt, pepper and a little sugar. Cook gently for 10 minutes, stirring all the time. Add two tablespoons finely chopped dill and 150ml (1/4 pint) sour cream. Heat very carefully, stirring all the time, do not bring to boil. Adjust seasoning, adding a little more sugar or lemon juice (or both) if necessary. Serve hot.

# Sauce Made with Hard-boiled Egg Yolks

Pass the yolks of two hard-boiled eggs through a sieve and mix to a smooth paste with a little French mustard, salt, pepper and vinegar. Gradually add sufficient oil to give the consistency of whipped cream, stirring all the time. Thin down with a little more vinegar, add about one tablespoon chopped chives and capers and blend well. Serve with cold meat – and if you can spare a tablespoon of good meat jelly, stir it in as well.

# Horseradish with Vinegar Dressing

*Essig Kren*

3 tablespoons finely grated
  horseradish
3 tablespoons oil

1 tablespoon vinegar
Pinch sugar, salt, pepper
2 tablespoons stock

Heat the stock and pour it over the grated horseradish. Leave to cool. Mix together all the other ingredients, whisk well, then fold in the horseradish. Serve with hot or cold meat.

# Horseradish Sauce I

*Krensauce*

Mix together four tablespoons cream, two tablespoons good wine vinegar, one teaspoon icing sugar and a pinch of salt. Stir in sufficient finely grated horseradish to give a thick and smooth consistency. Serve with cold meat.

# Horseradish Sauce II

*Mandelkren*

150ml (¼ pint) cream
30g (1oz) ground
  blanched almonds

1–2 heaped tablespoons
  horseradish
Pinch icing sugar

Whip cream until stiff, add a pinch of sugar and whisk until smooth. Fold in the ground almonds and the grated horseradish (quantity varies according to strength of horseradish and taste). Chill before serving. Very good with cold meat.

This is not really a sauce and much nearer to a sort of savoury mousse. It can be frozen in the icecube tray of a refrigerator (previously set at maximum freezing point) and served cut into slices.

*Austrian* cooking

# Caper Sauce

*Kapernsauce*

2 egg yolks
2 tablespoons olive oil
2 tablespoons wine vinegar
2 tablespoons water

2–3 lumps sugar
Salt, pepper
1 heaped tablespoon chopped
  capers

Dissolve the sugar in the vinegar, add all other ingredients except the chopped capers. Whisk over steam until thick, remove from heat and whisk until cool, then fold in the chopped capers.

# Tomato Sauce

*Paradeis Sauce*

500g (1lb) tomatoes
1 small carrot
1 onion
A little chopped parsley
  including some parsley root
Thyme

2 cloves
Sugar
Lemon juice or vinegar
Salt, pepper
1 tablespoon butter
1 tablespoon flour

Wash the tomatoes, do not dry them. Put tomatoes in a thick saucepan with very little water, cover with a lid and simmer until soft. Meanwhile slice onion and carrots and fry until golden brown in the fat. Add the chopped parsley, thyme, flour, cloves, salt, pepper, sugar and a little lemon juice or vinegar. Add the tomatoes, including the liquid in which they were cooked. Simmer for 10 minutes, then pass everything through a sieve. Serve hot.

# Cranberry Sauce

*Preiselbeersauce*

As the name implies, this should be made with cranberries – cranberry jelly, to be exact. If this is not available, redcurrant jelly can be used.

Mix four tablespoons of the melted jelly with one tablespoon rum, two tablespoons sherry, Madeira or Marsala and a little orange or lemon juice. Blend well and if you like the flavour of grated horseradish, add a small pinch of this. Otherwise stir in half a teaspoon French mustard – but on no account both. Nice with cold tongue, ham, game, in fact most cold meats – even corned beef.

# Anchovy Sauce I

*Sardellensauce I*

Rinse six boned anchovy fillets under cold running water. Shake a little to get rid of any water clinging to them, then chop them. Pound to a smooth paste with two heaped tablespoons butter. If no pestle and mortar are available, use a potato masher. Put the anchovy paste in a small bowl and stand it in hot water to melt, stir in the juice of half a lemon. Serve warm. Particularly favoured with pike or cooked pickled tongue. There is a short cut to the above recipe which does not quite produce the same result, but will do in an emergency: if there is no time to pound the anchovies, stir a tablespoon of good anchovy paste (sold in tubes at most grocer's) into the butter, then proceed as above.

# Anchovy Sauce II

*Sardellensauce II*

Fry one small finely chopped onion in one tablespoon butter. Dust with one tablespoon flour, add six finely scraped anchovies and stir. Add a large cup stock gradually and simmer for about 10 minutes. Just before serving stir in two tablespoons cream. If you like your sauces sharp, add also a pinch of freshly ground black pepper.

# Chives Sauce

*Schnittlauch Sauce*

Mix together two eggs, a quarter teaspoon flour and one tablespoon water, stir well. Bring about 90ml (3fl oz) water to boil, together with one tablespoon sugar, one tablespoon good wine vinegar and a pinch of salt and pepper. Pour the water over the eggs, whisking all the time. Return the mixture to the heat, cooking it in a double saucepan and stirring all the time until thick. Add another tablespoon vinegar, stir well and remove the sauce from the heat. Stir in two tablespoons good olive oil and a heaped tablespoon chopped chives. Serve warm.

# Mushroom Sauce

*Schwammerlsauce*

Served with dumplings, this makes a very satisfying main dish, but it is equally good when it accompanies meat. Clean and slice 250g (1/2 lb) mushrooms (or even mushroom stalks). Melt one heaped tablespoon butter, add the mushrooms, a small pinch caraway seeds, salt, pepper, and the juice of half a lemon. Sprinkle with chopped parsley and cover with a lid. Simmer gently for about 30 minutes until mushrooms are tender. Dust with one tablespoon flour, stir and add one ladleful clear stock. Simmer for 10 minutes, then stir in sufficient sour cream to give thick, creamy consistency. Heat, but do not let the sauce boil. Adjust seasoning and serve.

# Sauce for Boiled Beef

*Warme Rindfleisch Sauce*

When preparing boiled beef (see page 39), keep aside two tablespoons of the clear beef broth and make the following sauce to serve with the boiled beef:

Cut 90g (3oz) butter into small pieces and put them in a cup, stand the cup in hot water until the butter has softened. In a bowl over steam whisk together two egg yolks, three tablespoons cream, the broth and the juice of half a lemon. Add the softened butter gradually, whisking all the time. When the sauce begins to thicken, serve at once – it must not get really hot. A little salt may have to be added, but as a rule the seasoning of the stock combined with the sharpness of the lemon juice is all that is required.

# Onion Sauce

*Zwiebelsauce*

Melt one tablespoon butter or good lard, throw in three medium-sized onions cut into rings. Fry until pale golden brown, then add a good pinch of sugar and stir well. Fry for another minute or so, until onions are deep golden brown, add a ladleful of clear stock or water, a pinch of paprika, a dash of vinegar or lemon juice and a thick slice of brown bread (without crust). Let it boil up once, then pass everything through a sieve. Serve hot, either separately or poured over sliced meat. Salt to taste.

# *Dumplings and the Like*

# *Dumplings and the Like*

A *Knoedel* is a dumpling – sometimes large, sometimes smallish. A *Knoederl* is a small dumpling, used mainly in soups (see page 11). A *Nockerl* is tiny to medium-sized, oval in shape and not really a dumpling at all. The only reason why I continuously refer to them as such is for want of a better name. Perhaps it would be more correct to call them gnocchi, but that again would raise endless difficulties about *Gnocchi à la Romana* which are an entirely different thing altogether – so perhaps it's safer to stick to 'small dumplings'. There is a further point: in Austria *Nockerl* are made with the help of a *Nockerlbrett*, a thinnish piece of wood shaped in one with the handle. You hold it in your left hand and spread the paste over the wood. Small pieces of the paste are then cut off with a knife (dipped into hot water as you go along) and thrown straight into the boiling water or soup.

All very satisfactory – if you have a *Nockerlbrett*! Otherwise you will have to use the method prescribed on the following (and previous) pages of scooping out small balls with the help of a teaspoon – making the *Nockerl* look more and more like small dumplings...

# Dumplings made with Breadcrumbs

*Broeselknoedel*

125g (4oz) breadcrumbs
1 tablespoon flour
Salt

1 egg
1 tablespoon butter
Nutmeg

Cream butter, add the egg, salt and nutmeg. Beat in the breadcrumbs and the flour. Cover and leave to stand for 30 minutes. Form small dumplings and drop into boiling salt water. Cook for a few minutes only.

# Nockerl

Sift 250g (9oz) of flour into a bowl. Dissolve 30g (1oz) butter in 280ml (1/2 pint) of milk, do not bring to boil. Remove from heat as soon as butter has dissolved, add one egg and whisk until well blended. Salt to taste. Stir milk, etc., into flour until a stiff paste is obtained. Bring a large pan of water to boil, add a pinch of salt and cut out small dumplings with the help of a teaspoon, dipping spoon frequently into the boiling water. Cook for about 2 minutes, then fish out one of the small dumplings and taste. They require between 2 and 3 minutes' cooking time – no more. Drain in a colander or sieve, rinse dumplings under cold tap.

Melt one heaped tablespoon butter or dripping in a frying pan, add the *Nockerln* and heat carefully, shaking the pan from time to time. The *Nockerln* must not brown. Prepared this way, the *Nockerln* are ready to be served as an accompaniment to goulash, etc. For *Eiernockerl*, break 2 or 3 eggs into a bowl, salt and pepper to taste, and whisk lightly. Pour eggs over the *Nockerln* in the frying-pan and stir with a fork, rather like scrambling eggs. When eggs have set, stir again with a fork and serve at once, accompanied by a fresh green salad.

# Meat Dumplings

*Fleischknoedel*

Prepare paste as for *Zillertaler Krapfen* (see pages 94–5). Prepare a filling of equal quantities of finely ground pork and lean beef, a small chopped onion, pepper and salt. Bind with a little egg. Make small balls of the meat filling, wrap each ball with a thin cover of pastry. Drop dumplings into boiling-hot salt water, reduce heat and simmer for about 20 minutes. Drain, rinse with cold water and toss in hot fat to warm. Can be eaten with salad, Sauerkraut, in soup or in practically any other way.

# Semolina Dumplings

*Griessknoedel*

70g (2½oz) butter
1 tablespoon water
1 egg yolk

1 egg
Pinch salt
135g (5oz) coarse semolina

Cream butter, add the water gradually. Stir in the egg yolk and the lightly beaten egg together with 90g (3oz) semolina. Cover bowl and leave for 15 minutes. Add remaining semolina, leave to stand for 2 hours. Scoop out small balls with a tablespoon, handle very lightly and shape into dumplings. Drop into boiling salted water, cook until dumplings rise to the top. Drain, rinse under cold tap. Heat in sauce or gravy before serving.

# *Austrian* cooking

## *Pasta and Ham*

*Schinkenfleckerl*

Traditionally, these are made with little *Fleckerl* patches (see page 15) which should of course be home-made. Gastronomically, any good pasta is acceptable for this dish, provided it is small enough. This rules out macaroni, spaghetti, canelloni and the like, but *cornetti* (slightly curved, looking like broken-up macaroni and often erroneously sold as such), broad noodles and most of the *pastina minestrone* family sold in good shops (bows, rosettes, etc.) can be used. It is difficult to give exact quantities as this depends entirely on the pasta, but the recipe quoted below is for about 250g (8oz) of pasta. Cook the pasta in rapidly boiling salt water, being careful not to overcook it. Drain and rinse under cold tap. Butter a deep ovenproof dish. Cream one heaped tablespoon butter, beat in two egg yolks and gradually add 225ml (8fl oz) of sour cream and 125g (4oz) of chopped ham. Fold in two stiffly beaten egg whites and the drained pasta. Bake in the buttered casserole (190°C/375°F/Gas 5) until nicely browned on top. Serve with a green salad.

Again, as with most traditional recipes, there are numerous variations. You can just toss the cooked pasta in a little hot butter and leave out the 'creaming of butter', simply whisking together the sour cream and the egg yolks. The whipped eggwhites which are added at the end are also optional, leaving them out, however, gives a far less fluffy consistency.

## *Poor Knights filled with Calves Brains*

*Hirnpofesen*

Blanch a calf's brain, drain and remove the skin. Fry a small, finely chopped onion in a little fat until pale golden brown, add the brains, some chopped parsley, salt and pepper. Stir over low flame until the brains are cooked, add an egg and, still stirring, remove the pan from the heat. Cut a few thin slices of bread, using a French loaf if possible. Cut off the crusts. Dip the bread slices into milk for a second, then sandwich 2 and 2 together with the brain mixture. Press down a little and leave for about 10 minutes. Dip into seasoned, lightly beaten egg, then into breadcrumbs and fry golden brown on both sides. Serve with creamed spinach.

# Bread Dumplings I

*Semmelknoedel*

4 rolls
1 egg or 1 egg yolk
2–3 rashers bacon
  (optional)

chopped parsley
Fat
Flour
Salt, pepper

Use day-old rolls or an equivalent quantity of bread. Dice bread or rolls, chop the bacon. Fry the bacon lightly, add a little fat and brown the diced rolls in this. Break egg into a cup and fill up cup with milk. Mix milk and egg, add a pinch of salt and pepper. Empty contents of frying pan into bowl and pour over milk, etc., while diced bread is still warm. Stir in four heaped tablespoons flour and leave to stand for 30 minutea. Add chopped parsley and form dumplings, adding a little more flour if necessary, and drop into boiling salt water. Cook for 10 to 15 minutes. Good with goulash, Sauerkraut or brown lentils.

Left-over dumplings can be used up in the following way. Slice the cold dumplings thinly and fry them in a little fat. Pour over 1 or 2 lightly beaten eggs and treat as for scrambled eggs. Serve with a green salad. This is known simply as *Knoedel mit Ei* (dumplings with egg) and makes a very popular light luncheon dish.

# *Austrian* cooking

## *Dumpling Cooked in a Napkin*

*Serviettenknoedel*

250g (1/2 lb) cream cheese
60g (2oz) semolina
45g (1 1/2oz) butter

2 eggs
Salt and sugar

Separate egg yolks and whites. Cream butter with a pinch of salt and sugar, add egg yolks and semolina. Leave to stand for 2 hours. Fold in stiffly beaten eggwhites alternately with cream cheese. Form one large dumpling and place it in the centre of a napkin previously wrung out in cold water. Tie ends loosely over the dumpling. Have ready a pan of boiling water to which a pinch of salt has been added. Slot the handle of a wooden cooking spoon through the tied napkin ends and thus hang the dumpling into boiling water – resting the wooden handle on the saucepan rim. Cover saucepan with a lid and lower heat. Simmer the dumpling for 30 minutes. (Hanging the dumpling into the boiling water in the manner described above prevents it from sinking to the bottom of the pan and burning.)

This dumpling, sliced and sometimes sprinkled with breadcrumbs fried in butter, is served with meat instead of potatoes. Sliced and sprinkled with melted butter and sugar, it is served as a dessert, usually accompanied by stewed fruit.

## *Fried Meat Turnovers*

*Zillertaler Krapfen*

Sift 250g (1/2 lb) of flour on to a pastry board, add an egg (or egg yolk), salt and enough warm water to make a stiff paste. Knead well. Shape into a roll and cut off small pieces – about 2.5cm (1 in) long. Roll out each piece as thinly as possible. Prepare filling as follows: Cook 500g (1lb) of potatoes in their skins, peel and sieve while still hot. Add 250g (1/2lb) of cream cheese, an 140ml (1/4 pint) top milk, salt, pepper, one egg yolk, chopped chives or parsley and about 90g (3oz) of finely chopped ham or pork crackling. Stir in about one tablespoon flour to make a stiff paste. (More flour may be required, depending on the consistency of potatoes and cream cheese.) Put a good dab of this filling in centre of each pastry round, brush round filling with a little egg or milk, fold over and press together edges. Fry in smoking hot deep fat.

*Austrian* cooking

## Desserts, Hot and Cold
## including Sweet Sauces

# *Apple Snow*

*Apfelschnee*

2 large or 3 medium cooking
  apples
1 tablespoon lemon juice
3 eggs

4 tablespoons sugar
1 tumblerful white wine
1 teaspoon Maraschino
Sugar to taste

Separate egg yolks and whites. Wipe the apples and bake them in the oven until soft (180°C/350°F/Gas 4). Remove skin while still hot, mash the pulp and throw away the pips, etc. Put six tablespoons of this apple purée (about the result of the quantity of apples given), four tablespoons sugar, the lemon juice and the egg whites into a bowl and whisk over steam until thick. Using a rotary eggwhisk, this takes between 5 and 7 minutes. Remove from heat and add one teaspoon Maraschino. Continue whisking until cool. Cover the bowl and chill. Before serving, arrange the apple foam in a glass dish and serve very cold, with the following hot sauce handed separately:

Put the egg yolks, wine and sugar to taste (about three tablespoons) in a bowl and whisk over steam until thick. Serve at once.

# *Baked Pancakes with Vanilla Cream*

*Cremepalatschinken*

Prepare some pancakes as described on page 105. Sprinkle each pancake with grated walnuts and sugar and roll them up separately. Arrange pancakes side by side in a rectangular or oblong fireproof dish. Cook 280ml (½ pint) of milk with two egg yolks and about two tablespoons vanilla sugar in a double boiler until thick, pour over pancakes and bake in a medium oven at 180°C/350°F/Gas 4, until lightly browned.

# *Austrian* cooking

## *Pudding made with Sponge fingers and Wine*

*Biskotten Auflauf*

280ml (1/2 pint) white wine
200g (7oz) sugar
Juice 1 lemon
Jam

280ml (1/2 pint) milk
About 20 sponge fingers
2 eggs

Butter a deep pie-dish. Put the wine and the lemon juice in a saucepan, add 125g (5oz) sugar and stir over low heat until all the sugar has dissolved. Dip each sponge finger into the wine, arrange sponge fingers in layers in the pie-dish, putting small blobs of jam between each layer. Whisk the eggs lightly with the remaining sugar and a little cold milk, heat remaining milk and pour over the eggs. Whisk well, pour over sponge fingers in pie-dish and bake until golden brown (190°C/375°F/Gas 5).

## *Cream Pudding*

*Creme Pudding*

Whisk together 280ml (1/2 pint) of milk with a vanilla pod, three egg yolks, one tablespoon flour and 90g (3oz) of sugar over steam until fluffy. Butter a deep pie-dish and pour in a layer of this cream, about 1cm (1/2in), having first removed the vanilla pod. Cut some sponge cakes into slices, sprinkle with rum and sandwich 2 and 2 together with jam. Arrange the sponge slices in layers in the pie-dish, covering each layer with a little of the cream, finishing with a layer of the cream. Bake at 190°C/375°F/Gas 5 for 10 minutes. Meanwhile whisk the three whites until thick, whisk in two tablespoons castor sugar, then fold in a further three tablespoons castor sugar. Heap the whisked egg whites on top of the pudding and return it to the oven at 100°C/200°F/Gas 1/2 until meringue has set. Can be eaten hot or cold.

# 'Fried Mice'

*Gebackene Maeuse*

200g (7oz) flour
1 large or 2 small eggs
50g (2oz) butter
15g (½oz) sugar
10g (⅓oz) yeast

30g (1oz) raisins
1 tablespoon rum
⅛ litre (¼ pint) milk
Deep fat for frying

Separate egg yolks and whites. Wash and dry the raisins. Cream yeast with sugar, add a teaspoon of the flour and a little of the milk (tepid). Leave to prove in a warm place. Sift remaining flour into a bowl, make a well in the centre, drop in the egg yolk (or egg yolks), stir in the yeast, melted butter and remaining milk. Add the rum and mix well. Cover bowl with a cloth and leave to rise in a warm place. When the dough has risen to about twice the original size, fold in the stiffly beaten egg whites and the raisins. Drop tablespoons of the mixture into smoking hot deep fat, cover frying pan with a lid and fry until golden brown on one side. Turn over and fry other side (without a lid on the frying pan). Drain on paper, dust with sugar and serve hot with fruit syrup.

# 'Fried Straw'

*Gebackenes Stroh*

Make a smooth dough with ¾ cup flour, a pinch of salt, one tablespoon butter, one egg and, if necessary, a little milk. Knead well, then roll out as thinly as possible. Cut into noodles and drop into smoking hot fat. Fry until golden brown, drain on kitchen paper. Whisk ¼ litre (½ pint) of milk with two egg yolks and two tablespoons sugar over steam until thick. Arrange fried noodles in a deep pie-dish, sprinkle with 1 or 2 tablespoons washed and dried raisins and pour the egg cream over it. Brown in a hot oven for a few minutes.

# Semolina Cake Served as Sweet

*Griesstorte als Mehlspeise*

| | |
|---|---|
| 70g (2¹/2oz) sugar | 60g (2oz) ground almonds |
| 2 eggs | 30g (1oz) semolina |

SAUCE as for almond pudding (see page 122–3)

Butter and flour a cake tin. Separate egg yolks and whites. Whisk together sugar and egg yolks, fold in the ground almonds, stiffly beaten egg whites and the semolina – in that order. Pour mixture into cake tin and bake at 180°C/350°F/Gas 4 for about 30 minutes. Leave for a few minutes in the tin, then tip cake carefully into a dish. Pour the sauce over it and serve warm but not hot.

# *Kalter Reis*

It takes not a little bravery to quote a recipe which calls for 280ml (¹/2 pint) of cream and which, translated, means simply 'cold rice': both facts are enough to frighten anyone. In fact only a truly wonderful dish like this could manage to remain known under such a terrible name.

Wash 90g (3oz) of rice and cook it in 280ml (¹/2 pint) of milk with a vanilla pod and 60g (2oz) of sugar until soft, but not mushy. While still hot stir in 10g or 4 leaves of gelatine previously softened in a little water. Leave to cool and, just as the mixture begins to set, remove the vanilla pod and fold in 280ml (¹/2 pint) of whipped cream (a little less may be used). Arrange in a mould, rinsed in cold water, and chill thoroughly. Turn out on to a dish, surround with lightly stewed or fresh fruit (strawberries or raspberries) and pour over it a little raspberry syrup.

# 'Canaries Milk' *(Vanilla Custard)*

*Kananrienmilch*

A sweet sauce served with a number of puddings, etc.

| | |
|---|---|
| 1 egg yolk | Vanilla pod |
| 1/4 litre (1/2 pint) milk | 30g (1oz) sugar |

Heat the milk with the vanilla pod. Whisk together sugar and egg yolk, gradually add the warmed but not hot milk. Whisk over steam until very frothy. Use as required.

# *Bohemian Bun Pudding*

*Dampfnudeln*

| | |
|---|---|
| 60g (2oz) melted butter | About 75ml (1/8 pint) milk |
| 10g (1/3oz) yeast | Vanilla cream (see page 115) |
| 2 egg yolks | Milk |
| 1 heaped tablespoon sugar | A nut of butter and a little |
| 180g (6oz) flour | melted butter |

Cream yeast with a little of the sugar, add a teaspoon of the flour and some of the milk (tepid). Set in a warm place to prove. Sift remaining flour into a warmed bowl, add the egg yolks, 60g (2oz) melted butter, sugar, remaining milk and finally the yeast. Beat well with a wooden spoon until smooth. Cover with a cloth and set in a warm place to rise (about 45 minutes). Sprinkle a little flour on a pastry board, tip the dough on to the pastry board and lightly shape into a long roll. Cut off small rounds with a knife and set on a floured board to rise for 15 minutes in a warm place. Meanwhile preheat the oven to 190°C/375°F/Gas 5. Fill a baking dish 1cm (1/2in) deep with milk. Add a small nut of butter and heat it. Put the pastry rounds in the milk, packing them not too tightly and brushing the tops with some melted butter. Cover the baking dish with a lid and bake the 'noodles' in the oven, removing the lid towards the end of the baking time, so that the tops are nicely browned. The milk evaporates and the noodles are served hot, with vanilla cream (see page 115) poured over them.

# Chestnut Mont Blanc

*Kastanienreis*

Take about 500g (1lb) or more chestnuts and make a slit across the top. Place chestnuts on a baking sheet and put them in a hot oven (230°C/450°F/Gas 8) for a few minutes, until the shells come away easily. Have ready a saucepan with hot milk and a vanilla pod and drop chestnuts into milk as they are shelled (keep the chestnuts hot while shelling them, the skins are difficult to remove once the chestnuts have cooled). Simmer chestnuts in milk until soft. Drain, retaining the milk and rub chestnuts through a sieve. Cook 75ml (1/8 pint) of the milk with 90g (3oz) of sugar until sugar spins a small thread, pour over the sieved chestnuts and beat well with a wooden spoon. Put the cooled mixture into a potato ricer and force it through the ricer straight into a glass bowl or into individual sundae glasses. Put a generous blob of sweetened whipped cream in the centre and top with a glacé cherry.

# Hazel Nut Pudding with Hazel Nut Cream

*Haselnussauflauf mit Creme*

Butter a deep pie-dish and dust it with ground hazel nuts. Preheat oven to 190°C/375°F/Gas 5. Toast 100g (3oz) of hazel nuts on a baking sheet in the oven until skins come off easily. Rub off the skins and grind the hazel nuts. Separate yolks and whites of three eggs, set aside one of the yolks for the cream. Whisk the remaining two egg yolks with 30g (1oz) of sugar until thick, whisk three egg whites until stiff, whisk in 30g (1oz) of sugar. Fold egg whites into egg yolks, together with 70g (2oz) grated hazel nuts, 30g (1oz) of flour, a little grated lemon rind, 30g (1oz) of melted butter and a pinch of cinnamon. Bake in a pie-dish until top is nicely browned (190°C/375°F/Gas 5) and serve with the following sauce:

## *Haselnuss Creme (Hazel Nut Cream)*

Put the egg yolk, 1/4 litre (1/2 pint) of milk, one tablespoon sugar and a vanilla pod with one teaspoon flour on top of a double boiler. Blend until smooth and cook very carefully, stirring all the time, until thick. Stir in the remaining 30g (1oz) of hazel nuts and remove vanilla pod.

# *Pudding Made with Croissants*

*Kipfelkoch*

The original recipe calls for the typical Austrian croissants (*Kipfel*), but ordinary croissants will do very well indeed, provided they are 1 or 2 days old.

*5 croissants*
*A little milk*
*45g (1 1/2oz) butter*
*60g (2oz) sugar*

*15g (1/2oz) breadcrumbs*
*1 large egg*
*1 egg yolk*
*Lemon juice and rind*

Butter a soufflé dish or a deep pie-dish. Slice the croissants and soak in a little milk. Cream butter and sugar, add lemon juice and rind. Gradually add the egg and the egg yolk and the breadcrumbs, fold in the croissants. Arrange in the buttered dish and bake at 190°C/375°F/Gas 5 until nicely browned. Serve with stewed fruit.

# *Cherry Dessert*

*Kirschenmehlspeise*

Whisk together 2 cups sour milk and two eggs, stir in 1 cup coarse semolina and two tablespoons melted butter. Brush a baking dish well with melted butter, pour in the semolina mixture, sprinkle thickly with stoned cherries. Bake at 200°C/400°F/Gas 6 until nicely browned, cut into squares and serve, sprinkled thickly with sugar.

# *Austrian* cooking

# *Apricot Dumplings*

*Marillenknoedel*

For some reason, best known to themselves, the female members of my family maintained that plum dumplings should be made with a potato paste while for *Marillenknoedel* (apricot dumplings) the special kind of paste quoted below was obligatory. Explanations as to why this was so were not easily forthcoming, but it appeared to be a matter of seasons: when the plums are ripe, potatoes are usually of the right floury consistency for making potato paste. Which does not quite explain why the paste quoted for *Marillenknoedel* was never used for plum dumplings!

There is, of course, no reason why the pastes should not be switched and you might care to try the paste given on page 117 for the apricot dumplings quoted below.

Stone some apricots and replace the stone with a lump of sugar. This is best done by easing the stone out gently – with the help of a cooking spoon handle – without actually cutting open the apricots. Heat 420ml (3/4 pint) of water with a pinch of salt and a tablespoon butter. When the water boils, tip in 250g (1/2lb) of flour and stir over low heat until the dough leaves the sides of the pan clean. Remove from heat and beat in two eggs or two egg yolks, one after the other. Beat well with a wooden spoon until quite smooth, put the dough into a bowl or on a pastry board and leave to cool. When cold knead briefly just so that the dough should be smooth, then pinch off small pieces of dough and completely cover each apricot with dough, taking care that there should not be any gaps. Bring a large pan of water to the boil, add a pinch of salt and drop the dumplings into the boiling water 1 by 1. They will sink to the bottom at once, stir carefully so that they do not stick. Cover saucepan with a lid, leaving a small gap open. Cook gently – the dumplings will rise to the top when ready. Leave to simmer for another minute or two, then lift out the dumplings very carefully, set them in a colander or a sieve and rinse under cold water. Melt three tablespoons butter in a saucepan, add 125g (4oz) good breadcrumbs and fry them until nicely browned, stirring all the time. Add the dumplings and toss them in the crumbs over low heat. Arrange dumplings and crumbs on a warmed dish, sprinkle with sugar and serve.

# Pancakes

*Palatschinken*

1/4 litre (1/2 pint) milk
1 egg
Pinch salt

About 125g (4oz) flour
Butter or fat for frying

Sift flour and salt into a bowl, add egg and milk gradually and whisk briskly. Some cooks add a dash of soda water at this point – it does help, but if you have no soda water you will just have to whisk the batter a little more briskly. Have ready a small jug with melted fat or butter. Heat a frying pan, pour in a teaspoon of melted fat or butter, move the pan so that the fat is spread evenly, and when it gets smoking hot pour in a little of the batter. Move pan quickly so that the mixture spreads. Shake pan a little while one side of the pancake is frying, turn pancake over and fry the other side. Use up the rest of the batter in the same way, keeping the fried pancakes warm meanwhile. You can now use a number of fillings: apricot jam is perhaps the most usual, but grated nuts and sugar, grated chocolate and nuts are equally good. Spread (or sprinkle) the filling over each pancake, roll it up and arrange the pancakes on a warmed dish. Sprinkle with sugar and serve at once. Austrian pancakes are fatter than their English counterparts, and lemon – crimped or otherwise – is not served as a matter of course.

# Nuss Nudeln

Throw some noodles (the broad type, not vermicelli) into a large pan of boiling salt water and cook until just tender. Do not overcook, or they will be quite horrid. Drain in a colander and rinse under cold running water. Melt a tablespoon or more (depending on quantity of noodles) of butter in a saucepan and toss the noodles in this. They must not actually fry in the fat, but should be nicely covered with fat all over and thoroughly heated. Heap on a hot dish and sprinkle liberally with finely ground walnuts and sugar (mixed together). Serve at once, handing a bowl of grated walnuts and sugar separately.

*Mohn Nudeln* are precisely the same thing, using ground poppy seeds and sugar instead of the walnuts.

# *Austrian* cooking

# 'Poor Knights'

*Pofesen*

Trim or grate the crust off a two-day-old French loaf. Cut into slices the thickness of a finger, then cut down centre of each slice to within 3mm (1/8in) of edge and spread some nice firm jam into the opening. Dip slices into milk – or, better still, red or white wine – taking care that they should not get too wet. Dip each slice into lightly beaten egg or pancake batter (see page 105) and fry in smoking hot fat until golden brown on both sides. Drain and serve hot, dusted with sugar. Fruit syrup can be handed separately.

# Rice Pudding

*Reisauflauf*

175g (6oz) rice
Scant 1/2 litre (3/4 pint) milk
Vanilla pod
1 tablespoon butter

2 eggs
90g (3oz) sugar
Lemon rind
Raspberries or strawberries

Butter a soufflé dish. Wash the rice, put it in a saucepan with the butter, a vanilla pod, some lemon rind and cover with scant 1/2 litre (3/4 pint) of milk. Cook gently until rice is soft but not mushy. Remove from heat and leave to cool slightly. Separate egg yolks and whites. Whisk first the yolks with half the sugar until thick and creamy, then the whites until stiff. Whisk in remaining sugar. Fold egg whites into egg yolks. Remove vanilla pod and lemon rind from cooked rice. Fold egg mixture into rice, which should by now be just tepid. Pile half the rice into the soufflé dish, arrange a layer of strawberries or raspberries over it (dust with a little sugar) and top with remaining rice. Bake at 170–180°C/325°–350°F/Gas 3–4 until golden brown. Raspberry syrup should be handed separately.

There are a great many versions of this recipe: apples may be used instead of strawberries or raspberries, or you can leave out the fruit altogether but stir a small handful of washed and dried raisins into the rice before baking. (Incidentally, the cooking of the rice can be done quite some time before it is finished off for baking, in fact you can use up cold left-over rice pudding in this way.) If you can spare an extra egg white whisk it with 2 tablespoons of sugar and top the baked pudding with this, returning it to the oven at low heat for the meringue to set.

Yet another version is to cook the rice with the vanilla pod and the lemon rind, but without the butter. The butter is creamed separately (using about half a tablespoon more than stated in the recipe) with the sugar and the egg yolks and the whipped egg whites are then folded in. The mixture is folded into the cooked rice – remaining procedure and quantities as before. This gives a slightly more substantial pudding, frequently served with vanilla cream (see page 115).

# *Bread Pudding*

*Scheiterhaufen*

8 rolls
1/4 litre (1/2 pint) milk
1–2 eggs
60g (2oz) raisins
500g (1lb) apples

30g (1oz) chopped almonds or
   hazel nuts
90g (3oz) butter
90g (3oz) sugar

Slice the rolls – which should be at least one day old. Whisk together milk and egg (or eggs) and pour over the sliced rolls. Leave to stand while peeling, coring and slicing the apples. Sprinkle apples with the sugar, raisins and chopped almonds. Arrange the sliced rolls in layers in a deep buttered pie-dish, spreading the apple mixture between each layer and dotting with butter. Finish with a layer of sliced rolls, dot with butter and bake at 190°C/375°F/Gas 5 until golden brown.

*Austrian* cooking

# Salzburger Nockerl

Quantities for two people:

3 eggs (ideally this should
  be 3 egg yolks and 4 egg
  whites)

1 teaspoon icing sugar
1 teaspoon flour
1 tablespoon butter

Preheat the oven to 270°C/525°F/Gas 9. Put an ovenproof omelette pan over a low heat. Separate egg yolks and whites. Whisk the egg yolks very lightly with a fork until well blended. Whisk egg whites until very stiff, add the icing sugar and whisk until smooth. Fold the egg yolks into the egg whites – not the other way round as is more usual with other recipes – then fold in the flour. Put the butter in the omelette pan and turn up the heat. The butter should melt at once. Wait until the butter foams, then drop the soufflé mixture in three large 'blobs' into the hot butter. Make the blobs high rather than wide and set them a little apart. Leave over medium heat until underneath parts of the *Nockerln* have set – about 30 seconds – then push the omelette pan quickly into the hot oven. Leave until tops of *Nockerln* have browned lightly (this again is a matter of minutes).

    Dust liberally with icing sugar and serve at once. The centre should be light and creamy, the outside golden brown and puffed.

# 'Locksmith's Apprentices'
## (Prune Fritters)

*Schlosserbuben*

| | |
|---|---|
| 1/8 litre (1/4 pint) beer | Salt |
| 125g (4 1/2oz) flour | Prunes |
| 1 teaspoon oil | Blanched almonds |
| 1 egg | Grated chocolate |
| 15g (1/2oz) sugar | Deep fat for frying |

Soak the prunes in weak cold tea for 1 hour, remove the stones and replace them with blanched almonds. Separate egg yolk and white. Sift flour, salt and sugar into a bowl, blend with the egg yolk, oil and beer. Whisk the egg white until stiff, fold into the mixture.

Coat each prune with batter and drop into smoking hot fat, fry until golden brown. Drain on paper and serve sprinkled with grated chocolate.

# Schmarrn

*Schmarrn* means a mere nothing; a trifle tossed off easily; a favour denied.

Culinary *Schmarrn* are different. They are not trifles, but they are delicious. *Kaiserschmarrn* and *Griess Schmarrn* are perhaps the best known of all, but there is also *Semmelschmarrn* (made from bread rolls) and *Kipfelschmarrn*, built on a basis of croissants.

Tastes differ – you may like your *Schmarrn* soft or crisped almost to a frazzle. There is nothing like trying and tasting – and you have the wonderful consolation that nothing, absolutely nothing, can ever go wrong with a *Schmarrn*!

# *Austrian* cooking

# *Kaiserschmarrn*

1/8 litre (1/4 pint) milk
90g (3oz) flour
2 eggs

25g (1oz) raisins
1/2 tablespoon sugar
1 heaped tablespoon butter

Wash and dry the raisins. Preheat the oven to 200°C/400°F/Gas 6.
Separate egg yolks and whites. Sift flour and sugar into a bowl and stir in
the milk gradually using as much 'top of the bottle' as you can spare. Add
the egg yolks and blend well; the mixture must be very smooth. Fold in the
stiffly beaten egg whites. Melt the butter in a baking dish and when it begins
to foam, pour in the batter and sprinkle the raisins over the top. The batter
should be about 2.5cm (1in) deep in the baking dish. Bake in the oven until
nicely browned, pondering meanwhile over the question whether you want
your *Kaiserschmarrn* very crisp or just a little soft. If you want it very crisp,
turn it over completely with a fish slice as soon as one side is brown – it
doesn't matter if it breaks in the process – and return it to the oven for a few
minutes so that there is a nice crust top and bottom, then tear it into small
pieces with two forks and return it to the oven for another minute or two.
Serve on a hot dish, sprinkled with vanilla sugar. If you want it just a little
softer, do not turn it over, but tear it into small pieces as soon as it is
browned on one side, return it to the oven for a little longer and serve dusted
with icing sugar as described before.

# Griess Schmarrn

Scant 1/2 litre (3/4 pint) milk
150–170g (5–6oz) coarse semolina
2 tablespoons butter

Vanilla pod
15g (1/2oz) sugar
1 heaped tablespoon raisins

Put the milk, vanilla pod, sugar and a small knob of butter in a saucepan and bring to boil. Rain in the semolina, stirring constantly. Add the raisins, switch off the heat and cover the saucepan, leave it to stand for about 5 minutes. Meanwhile melt the remaining butter in a baking dish, pour in the semolina mixture and put it in the oven (190°C/375°F/Gas 5). As soon as the mixture is nicely browned on top, tear it into small pieces with two forks. Return it to the oven so that the whole thing should crisp nicely, then turn it on to a warmed dish and sprinkle liberally with icing sugar. The vanilla pod can be removed either before or after the baking.

# ~Austrian~ cooking

## Snowballs

*Schneeballen*

Serve them with a little raspberry syrup as a sweet, or just sprinkled with icing sugar and a pinch of cinnamon, they will grace your tea table. The recipe for *Rosenkrapfen* (see page 154) may be used for the pastry. If you can spare an extra egg yolk, however, there is a very luxurious version:

| | |
|---|---|
| 90g (4oz) flour | 30ml (1fl oz) white wine |
| 50g (2oz) butter | A few drops rum |
| 3 egg yolks | Deep fat for frying |
| 1/2 tablespoon cream | |

Sift the flour on to the pastry board, make a well in the centre and gradually add the liquid ingredients. Work to a smooth dough with the butter, cover with a cloth and leave for 30 minutes. Roll out to about 3mm (1/8in) thickness, cut into small rectangles, using a zig-zag pastry cutter. The rectangles should measure about 10 x 7.5cm (4 x 3in). Run the pastry cutter 3 or 4 times down each rectangle, from within 1cm (1/2in) of the edge to 1cm (1/2in) of the opposite edge. Heat the fat and, when smoking hot, drop in each snowball separately, picking up alternate strips with the handle of a wooden cooking spoon, thus letting each 'snowball' slide into the hot fat. Fry until golden brown, drain on crumpled kitchen paper and dust with icing sugar while still hot. Serve as soon as possible after frying.

## Floating Islands

*Scheenockerl*

Whisk four egg whites until stiff. Gradually whisk in four tablespoons sifted icing sugar. The mixture must be very stiff and smooth. In a large saucepan (ideally a frying pan with a lid) heat scant 1/2 litre (3/4 pint) of milk with 1/8 litre (1/4 pint) of water and a vanilla pod. When the milk begins to rise, lower heat at once and drop in the egg white mixture with the help of a tablespoon, taking care that the *Nockerl* do not touch as they swell during the cooking. Cover with a lid and simmer gently for 3 minutes, the milk must

112

not boil. Remove lid, carefully turn the *Nockerl* with a palette knife and simmer for another minute or two – this time minus the lid. Lift out the *Nockerl* with a perforated spoon and arrange them in a dish. Use up remaining egg white mixture in the same way. Measure liquid in which the *Nockerl* were cooked and make it up to scant 1/2 litre (3/4 pint) with milk. Add 90g (3oz) of sugar and heat. Slake 25g (1scant oz) of flour with 1/2 cup cold milk, whisk in three egg yolks. Gradually pour on the hot milk. Cook in a double boiler stirring constantly, until thick. Remove vanilla pod, pour the cream over the *Nockerl* and chill well before serving.

# Pudding Made with Rolls

*Semmel Auflauf*

| | |
|---|---|
| 2 rolls | 25g (1 tablespoon) raisins |
| 70g (2 1/2oz) butter | 2 eggs |
| 40g (1 1/2oz) sugar | Lemon rind and juice |
| 40g (1 1/2oz) ground walnuts | Milk |

Use rolls at least two days old. Grate off the crust and set aside one tablespoon of the fine breadcrumbs that result. Wash and dry the raisins. Soak the rolls in milk until soft, squeeze out all moisture. Cream butter and sugar, add the egg yolks gradually, then the rolls, raisins and the ground walnuts. Fold in the stiffly beaten egg whites, lemon rind and juice and finally one tablespoon breadcrumbs. Bake until golden brown (190°C/375°F/Gas 5) in a buttered soufflé or pie-dish.

# Stephanie Omelette

(Quantity sufficient for three moderate or two greedy people.)

3 eggs
2 tablespoons icing sugar
2 tablespoons flour

3 tablespoons cream
1 tablespoon butter
Apricot jam

Preheat the oven to 220°C/425°F/Gas 7. Set an ovenproof omelette pan over a low heat. Separate egg yolks and whites. Whisk egg yolks, cream and sugar unil pale and creamy, whip egg whites until stiff. Fold egg whites into egg yolks, carefully add the flour. Melt butter in the omelette pan, do not let it foam – as soon as it is melted turn the pan round and round so that bottom and sides are well covered with the melted butter. Put the omelette mixture into the pan, spreading it so that it is slightly higher round the sides – this makes the folding over easier. Put the omelette into the hot oven as quickly as possible and leave to brown. This takes about 8 minutes, by which time the omelette should be nicely puffed up and golden brown. Spread quickly with warmed apricot jam and slide on to a sugared, warmed dish, folding the omelette over at the same time. Dust top with sugar and serve at once. Sugared strawberries or raspberries, with a dash of Kirsch, also make an excellent filling.

# Cream Cheese Turn-overs

*Topfentascherl*

Prepare a stiff paste with 200g (7oz) flour, one egg, salt and about 75ml (⅛ pint) of water. Roll out thinly and stamp into rounds. Cream 75g (2½oz) of butter with one heaped tablespoon sugar, add one egg, 125–175g (4–6oz) of cream cheese, and sufficient milk or sour milk to give a stiff paste. Stir in a few washed and dried raisins. Put a good dab of filling in centre of each pastry round, brush round the filling with egg and fold over pastry, pressing down the edges. Cook in boiling salt water for about 8 minutes, drain and rinse under cold tap. Toss in hot butter and sprinkle thickly with sugar and cinnamon before serving.

# Vanilla Cream

*Vanille Creme*

To be served with hot or cold puddings.

Scant ½ litre (3/4 pint) milk
Vanilla pod
1 tablespoon cornflour

2 egg yolks or 1 whole egg
75g (3oz) sugar

Whisk together sugar, egg yolks, cornflour and a little of the cold milk. Heat remaining milk with the vanilla pod and pour over other ingredients, stirring all the time. Return mixture to stove in a double boiler and cook until thick, stirring all the time. Remove vanilla pod before serving.

Austrian cooking

# Wine Pudding

*Weinkoch*

A good substantial sweet for a cold day – quantities may be halved if necessary.

4 eggs
60g (2oz) ground unblanched
  almonds

60g (2oz) sugar
30g (1oz) biscuit crumbs
Grated lemon rind

## also

1/8 litre (1/4 pint) white wine
Vanilla pod
70g (2½oz) sugar

1 clove
Juice and rind of 1/2 lemon
1/8 litre (1/4 pint) water

Butter a deep pie-dish and sprinkle it with ground almonds. Separate egg yolks and whites. Whisk egg yolks with one 30g (1oz) of sugar until thick and creamy. Whisk egg whites until stiff, fold in the remaining 30g (1oz) of sugar and whisk again. Fold egg whites into egg yolks, fold in the ground almonds and the crumbs, sprinkle in the grated lemon rind. Bake at 200°C/400°F/Gas 6 until nicely browned (about 20 to 25 minutes). While the pudding is baking, put 70g (2½oz) of sugar in a saucepan and melt over a low heat. When the sugar turns pale yellow, add the wine, water, vanilla pod, clove, lemon juice and rind. Heat well and strain hot over the baked pudding. Serve at once.

# 'Viennese Pudding'

*Wiener Koch*

200ml (7fl oz) milk
3 eggs
45g (1½oz) butter

60g (2oz) vanilla sugar
1 tablespoon flour

Preheat oven to 220°C/425°F/Gas 7 and prepare a soufflé dish as described on page 118. Separate egg yolks and whites. Blend together flour and egg yolks, add a little cold milk. Heat remaining milk with the butter and stir into egg yolks, etc. Return mixture to stove in a double boiler and cook very gently, stirring constantly until thick. Remove from heat, stir until cool. Fold in stiffly beaten egg whites and bake for about 12 minutes.

# Plum Dumplings

### Zwetschkenknoedel

Use the small blue plums which look rather like outsize damsons. Some Soho greengrocer's even sell them under the name *Zwetschken*. Stone the plums and replace the stone with a lump of sugar.

Boil 500g (1lb) of potatoes in their skins, using floury potatoes. Skin while still hot and push them through a sieve straight onto the pastry board. Leave to cool, then add a pinch of salt, one egg (or two egg yolks), two tablespoons butter and sufficient flour to make a dough which does not stick to the pastry board. The quantity of the flour varies according to the quality of potatoes, it may be anything between 150–250g (5–8oz) and it is therefore absolutely necessary to make a test with one dumpling before covering all the plums with dough. Cover the dough with a cloth and leave for 30 minutes. Pinch a small piece off the dough and wrap it round a plum, being careful that there are no gaps. Drop it into a large pan of boiling salted water, see that it does not stick to the bottom of the pan, and cover the pan with a lid, leaving a small gap open. The dumpling will rise to the top when cooked. Fish it out with a perforated spoon and cut it open. If the dough was too soft, add a little more flour (or fine semolina). If it was too stiff, work in a little more egg. Cover each plum with a little of the dough, carefully sealing all openings. Roll each dumpling between the palms of your hands to ensure it is quite smooth. Drop dumplings into boiling salted water, stir so that they do not stick to the bottom of the pan and cook gently until dumplings rise to the top (this takes about 10 to 12 minutes according to size). Cook in a covered saucepan, with the lid slightly tilted. Simmer for another minute after dumplings have risen to the top, then drain in a colander or a sieve, rinse under cold water. Melt three good tablespoons butter in a saucepan, stir in 120g (4oz) of breadcrumbs and brown. Add the dumplings and toss them in the breadcrumbs over a small flame. Arrange dumplings on a hot dish, sprinkle with sugar and serve.

# *Baked Soufflés*

## To Prepare a Soufflé Dish

Butter the dish well, then tie a piece of buttered paper round it to come about 5cm (2in) over the top. Dust the soufflé dish – including the paper – with icing sugar. For the Strawberry Soufflé I like to substitute ground almonds or hazel nuts for the sugar. The paper is of course removed just before serving and – need I say it – soufflés are best consumed within a one yard radius of the oven in which they were cooked!

## Cautionary Warning

With soufflés, almost more than with any other kind of dish, the idiosyncrasies of one's oven are important and simply have to be studied. Times and temperatures given apply to my own oven and you may find that they have to be varied slightly when applied elsewhere.

# *'Ladies Soufflé'*

*Damen Auflauf*

Prepare a soufflé dish as described above and preheat the oven to 220°C/425°F/Gas 7. Break 30g (1oz) of vanilla chocolate into small pieces and put in a warm place to melt. Separate yolks and whites of three eggs. Whisk the egg yolks with 75g (2½oz) of icing sugar, add the melted chocolate and finally fold in the stiffly beaten whites of the three eggs. Bake for about 12 minutes and serve at once – with hot chocolate sauce, if you are really greedy.

# Strawberry Soufflé

*Erdbeer Auflauf*

Preheat oven to 220°C/425°F/Gas 7 and prepare soufflé mould as described above. Put 90–100g (3oz) of unsweetened strawberry purée (made from about 150g (5oz) of fresh strawberries crushed through a sieve), 75g (2½oz) of granulated sugar and one egg white in a bowl. Stir, like creaming butter and sugar for a cake, until the mixture is thick and almost stiff. Whisk three egg whites until stiff, fold in one tablespoon granulated sugar, whisk for another minute until smooth. Fold whipped egg whites into strawberry mixture, fold in ½ tablespoon of flour and pile into the soufflé mould. Sprinkle with a few ground almonds or hazel nuts and bake at preset temperature for 10 minutes, then turn down heat to 195°C/385°F/Gas 5½ without opening oven door. Bake for another 7 minutes, serve at once.

# Soufflé Rothschild

Quantity for two persons:

| | |
|---|---|
| ⅛ litre (¼ pint) milk | 2 egg yolks |
| Vanilla pod | 3 egg whites |
| 1 tablespoon butter | 90g (3oz) glacé fruits |
| 2 tablespoons sugar | A little Kirsch |
| 45g (1½oz) flour | |

Preheat oven to 220°C/425°F/Gas 7 and prepare a soufflé dish as described on page 118. Put milk, one tablespoon sugar and one tablespoon butter in a saucepan, add a vanilla pod and bring to boil. Cut the glacé fruit into equal-sized chunks and moisten with a little Kirsch. When the milk boils, take out the vanilla pod and quickly stir in the flour, stirring the mixture over a low heat until it leaves the sides of the saucepan clean. Remove from heat, gradually beat in the egg yolks and when cool, fold in the egg whites whipped up stiff with the remaining sugar, and finally the glacé fruit. Pile into the soufflé dish and bake for about 10 to 12 minutes. Serve with vanilla cream (see page 115).

# Lemon Soufflé

*Zitronen Auflauf*

Preheat the oven to 200°C/400°F/Gas 6 and prepare a soufflé mould as described on page 118, dusting it very well with icing sugar. Separate yolks and whites of five eggs. Whisk the yolks with 85g (3oz) of icing sugar and the juice and grated rind of one lemon. When thick and creamy, fold in the stiffly beaten whites of five eggs. Pile into the soufflé dish and bake for about 12 minutes. Dust with icing sugar, remove paper and serve at once.

# Steamed Puddings

Whether you prefer to make one large pudding or divide the mixture into several small moulds is a matter of taste — and convenience. The mould (or moulds) must be well buttered, then sprinkled with sugar or ground hazel nuts, almonds or fine crumbs. This is infinitely preferable to flouring the mould. Never fill the moulds more than three-quarters full. Special moulds for steamed puddings are now sold which have a well-fitting lid. This is not really necessary, as long as the lid of the steamer fits well, but I always put a round of buttered paper on top of the pudding mixture to stop any condensed steam dripping into the pudding.

# Yellow Pudding with Chocolate Sauce

*Gelber Pudding mit Schokolade Sauce*

100g (3¹/2oz) butter
3 eggs
120g (4oz) sugar

Rind and juice of ¹/4 lemon
3 tablespoons flour

Separate egg yolks and whites. Cream butter and sugar, add yolks gradually. Fold in flour alternately with stiffly beaten egg whites. Add lemon rind and juice. Steam for about 45 minutes to 1 hour. Serve with the following sauce.

## Chocolate Sauce

*Schokolade Sauce*

Break 140g (4oz) of plain chocolate into small pieces. Dissolve chocolate in 280ml (¹/2 pint) of water together with 140g (4oz) of sugar and cook until thickened. Serve separately.

# Hazel Nut Pudding

*Haselnuss Pudding*

3 eggs
60g (2oz) butter
60g (2oz) sugar
60g (2oz) hazel nuts

30g (1oz) biscuit crumbs
30g (1oz) flour
Grated lemon rind

Separate egg yolks and whites. Cream butter with half the sugar. Beat in the egg yolks gradually. Whisk egg whites until stiff, whisk in remaining sugar. Fold egg whites into butter, add ground hazel nuts, crumbs and flour. Stir in grated lemon rind. Steam as described on page 120. Prepare the following sauce:

### Hazel Nut and Rum Sauce

1/4 litre (1/2 pint) milk
2 egg yolks
60g (2oz) sugar

60g (2oz) toasted hazel nuts
1 tablespoon rum

Place all ingredients except the hazel nuts in a bowl and whisk over steam until thick. Remove from heat and stir in ground hazel nuts. Hand sauce separately.

# Coffee Pudding

*Kaffeepudding*

80g (3oz) rolls (weight
  after cutting off crusts)
1/8 litre (1/4 pint) strong black coffee
80g (3oz) butter

3 eggs
80g (3oz) icing sugar
70g (2 1/2oz) ground almonds
  (not blanched)

Pour hot black coffee over rolls, stir well, then pass through a sieve. Separate egg yolks and whites. Cream butter with sugar, add egg yolks and rolls. Fold in stiffly beaten egg whites alternately with the ground almonds. Steam for about 45 minutes. Serve with wine sauce as for almond pudding (below).

# Almond Pudding

*Mandel Pudding*

4 eggs
70g (2 1/2oz) sugar
50g (2oz) flour

70g (2 1/2oz) ground almonds
30g (1oz) melted butter

Separate egg yolks and whites. Whisk yolks with half the sugar until fluffy. Whisk egg whites until stiff. Fold remaining sugar into egg whites, then fold whites into yolks, alternately with flour and ground almonds. Fold in melted butter. Steam for about 20 to 25 minutes. Serve with the following sauce:

## White Wine Sauce

1/8 litre (1/4 pint) white wine
2 eggs

Juice of 1/2 lemon
70g (2¹/2oz) sugar

Put all ingredients in a bowl and whisk over steam until light and bubbly.
Serve separately.

# Mohr Im Hemd

4 eggs
70g (2¹/2oz) butter
70g (2¹/2oz) sugar

70g (2¹/2oz) chocolate
70g (2¹/2oz) ground almonds

Butter pudding mould and dust with icing sugar. Separate egg yolks and
whites. Cream butter with sugar until light and fluffy. Beat in egg yolks one
after the other. Whip egg whites until stiff. Fold whipped egg whites into
creamed butter, alternately with the ground almonds and grated chocolate.
Fill into prepared mould. Steam for about 40 minutes. Should be served with
sweetened whipped cream – on special occasions with chocolate sauce (see
Yellow Pudding, page 121) and whipped cream. Can be eaten hot or cold.

# Nut Pudding

*Nusspudding*

4 eggs
140g (5oz) ground walnuts
1 heaped tablespoon fine
  breadcrumbs
70g (2½oz) sugar

100g (3oz) butter
2 small brioches
A tiny pinch powdered instant coffee
A little milk

If the brioches (day-old for preference) are not available, a small roll, minus the crust, will do. Prepare a pudding basin as described on page 000. Separate egg yolks and whites. Soak the brioches (or roll) in milk until soft, squeeze out the moisture and crumble between the fingers. Cream butter and sugar, add the egg yolks and the crumbled brioches. Fold in stiffly whipped egg whites, ground walnuts, breadcrumbs and a tiny pinch powdered instant coffee. Steam in pudding mould as described on page 120. Serve with whipped cream or fruit syrup.

# Rum Pudding

*Rum Pudding*

70g (2½oz) butter
70g (2½oz) sugar
3 eggs
70g (2½oz) ground almonds
  (not blanched)

70g (2½oz) raisins
30g (1oz) chocolate
20g (1 scant oz) breadcrumbs,
  moistened with rum

Separate egg yolks and whites. Cream butter and sugar, add egg yolks gradually. Fold in stiffly whipped egg whites alternately with ground almonds, chocolate and crumbs. Stir in raisins. Steam for about 45 minutes.

## Rum Sauce

Whisk over steam three tablespoons rum, two egg yolks and a little sugar until frothy. Pour over pudding or hand separately.

# Chocolate Pudding

*Schokolade Pudding*

50g (2oz) butter
40g (1½oz) sugar
35g (1½oz) toasted ground
  almonds

3 eggs
1½ rolls
25g (1oz) chocolate
milk

Cut crusts off rolls, cut rolls into cubes and soak in milk. Separate egg yolks and whites. Cream butter and sugar, add egg yolks gradually. Drain rolls, squeeze out moisture and add. Whisk egg whites until stiff, fold into mixture, also fold in grated chocolate and ground almonds. Steam for about 45 minutes.

To lift this pudding right into the luxury class, serve with the following:

## Chocolate Sauce with Whipped Cream

Break 125g (4oz) of chocolate into small pieces and melt in oven. Melt four tablespoons sugar in two tablespoons water and cook to 'small thread' stage. Remove from heat and stir into melted chocolate. Stir until cool, but still spreadable, then fold in 140ml (¼ pint) of whipped cream.

*Austrian* cooking

## Cakes, Pastries
## and Biscuits

# Cakes, Pastries and Biscuits

The culinary repertoire of Austria boasts many cake and biscuit recipes. Some are rich and rare and require an army of helpers to reach perfection. Others are so simple that it seems presumptuous even to write down the recipe. Most of them are widely known and where this is the case, there are also many variations regarding the preparation of one and the same thing. Thus there are numerous recipes concerning *Guglhupf*, or *Bischofsbrot*, or the hundred and one different yet similar nut and almond biscuits.

I have tried to be discriminating and yet fair to recipes which I have known and loved since I can remember. If I have seemingly repeated myself – it was done in the firm belief that a box overflowing with home-made biscuits is better than all the shop-bought cakes in the world!

# Apple Flan

*Apfel Pastete*

Sift together 50g (2oz) of sugar and 140g (5oz) of flour. Crumble 140g (5oz) of butter into the sugar and flour, add 70g (2½oz) of ground almonds (unblanched), a few drops lemon juice and one whole egg. Pat into a round and chill for 30 minutes. Line bottom and sides of a buttered and floured sandwich tin with this pastry, bake 'blind' (190°C/375°F/Gas 5). Meanwhile peel and slice three apples and put the slices in a saucepan. Dust with sugar, add a few raisins, about one tablespoon ground and blanched almonds and a dash of rum. Simmer very gently – using no water – for about 5 minutes. Remove from stove and leave to cool. Whisk one large egg white until stiff, add 25g (1oz) castor sugar, whisk again until smooth. Fold in another 40g (1½oz) of castor sugar. Fill pastry shell with the apples and with a forcing bag pipe a criss-cross pattern of the meringue mixture over the top. Put in a cool oven (130°C/250°F/Gas 1) until meringue has set.

# Apple Slices

*Apfelschnitten*

Prepare a short crust with 250g (9oz) of flour, 170g (6oz) of butter, three tablespoons sugar, three tablespoons top milk, one egg yolk and a little grated lemon rind. Divide pastry into two equal parts and chill for 15 minutes. After that time, knead pastry a little so that it is perfectly smooth, roll out on a floured pastry board into two equal-sized pieces. Put one sheet of pastry on a buttered and floured baking sheet, cover thickly with sliced apples, sprinkle with sugar and raisins and place other sheet of pastry on top. Prick lightly with a fork, brush with egg white and bake until golden brown (185°C/360°F/Gas 4½). Cut into slices when cold and dust with icing sugar.

# *Apple Strudel*

*Apfelstrudel*

Strudel pastry as described on
  page 159
FILLING
500g (1lb) cooking apples
3/4 cup raisins

1 cup sugar
1 1/2 cups breadcrumbs
Butter for frying
Apricot jam
Melted butter

Prepare strudel pastry as described on page 159. Peel, core and thinly slice the apples. Add the raisins to the apples, sprinkle with sugar. Set aside in a bowl and cover it. Fry breadcrumbs in butter. Sprinkle the fried breadcrumbs evenly over the pastry, then spread the apple and raisin filling over half the surface only, sprinkle with melted butter and dot with a little apricot jam. Tear off the rather thick rim which overhangs the table and start rolling the strudel by lifting the cloth at the 'apple' end. Roll up very carefully, like a Swiss roll, close up ends and place on a buttered baking sheet, forming a horseshoe. Brush with melted butter and cover with greaseproof paper. Bake in the oven at 180–185°C/350–366°F/Gas 4–4 1/2 for about 45 minutes, removing paper towards the end. Sprinkle with vanilla sugar while still warm.

# *Bishop's Bread I*

*Bischofsbrot I*

3 eggs and their weight in
  sugar and flour
50g (2oz) dried figs
50g (2oz) walnuts
50g (2oz) dates

50g (2oz) unblanched almonds
50g (2oz) hazel nuts
50g (2oz) candied peel
A little lemon juice and
  grated lemon rind

Chop fruit and nuts. Separate egg yolks and whites. Whisk egg yolks with sugar, fold in the stiffly beaten egg whites alternately with the flour. Finally fold in lemon juice, lemon rind and fruit and nuts. Bake in an oblong buttered and floured cake tin (185°C/360°F/Gas 4 1/2). Cool on a rack and cut into thin slices when cold.

# Bishop's Bread II

*Bischofsbrot II*

2 eggs
100g (3½oz) butter
100g (3½oz) flour
100g (3½oz) sugar
45g (2oz) glacé cheries

45g (2oz) washed and dried
   raisins
45g (2oz) chocolate
45g (2oz) almonds or walnuts
A little grated lemon rind

Separate egg yolks and whites. Chop chocolate and almonds. (Chocolate can also be broken into small lumps.) Cream butter with half the sugar, add the egg yolks and cream well. Whisk egg whites until stiff, whisk in remaining sugar. Fold beaten egg whites into egg yolks alternately with the flour. Add lemon rind, raisins, almonds, glace cherries and chocolate gradually and bake in a buttered and floured oblong tin (180°C/350°F/Gas 4) for about 45 minutes. Cool on a rack and slice when cold.

# 'Bee's Sting'

*Bienenstich*

250g (9oz) flour
100g (3½oz) butter
45g (1½oz) sugar
3 tablespoons milk

100g (3½oz) butter
100g (3½oz) vanilla sugar
60g (2oz) ground almonds
Pinch baking powder

Sift together flour, sugar and baking powder. Work to a dough with the butter and the milk. Pat into a round and cover with a cloth.

    Melt the butter over a low heat until it begins to get 'oily'. Stir in the ground almonds and the vanilla sugar and continue stirring over low heat until the mixture is smooth and creamy. Remove from heat, stir until cool. Roll out the dough to a thickness of 6mm (¼in). Line a buttered and floured baking sheet with the pastry, spread the almond mixture over it and bake at 180°C/350°F/Gas 4 for about 35 minutes.

    *Note: A foundation of yeast pastry is sometimes used in place of the pastry quoted above – cut once and filled with vanilla cream and topped as described before.*

# Puff Pastry

*Blaetterteig*

No two cooks will ever quite agree about the way to make puff pastry. The method quoted below (cribbed by my grandmother from a retired patissier who came to live in our village) has two virtues: it is comparatively quick (as puff pastry goes, and not counting the 'resting' times) and safe. And what more can one want?

250g (9oz) flour
250g (9oz) butter
About 140ml (1/4 pint) water

1 tablespoon lemon juice or
  white wine vinegar
Pinch salt

(Our friend the patissier used dry white wine instead of lemon juice and water.)
     Sift together flour and salt. Crumble the butter into 85g (3oz) of flour, knead until smooth. Shape into a brick, trim off edges with a knife and keep the trimmings on one side. Cover the butter brick with a cloth wrung out in cold water, set it aside in a cool place, but do not put in a refrigerator. Sift the remaining 165g (6oz) of flour on to a pastry board, make a well in the centre and pour in a little of the water and the lemon juice. Draw the flour towards the middle, gradually adding the remaining water. Add the trimmings from the butter brick and knead really well until dough is very smooth and pliable. Pat into a round, make a cross-like incision on top with a knife, cover with a cloth wrung out in cold water and leave for 30 minutes. After that time roll it out on a very lightly floured pastry board to a strip three times as long and about 5cm (2in) wider than the butter brick. The pastry should be slightly thicker in the middle, tapering off towards the sides. Place butter brick in centre, fold edges over so that the brick is completely covered with pastry and beat with a rolling pin from the centre outwards, then roll into a strip. (Some cooks prefer to roll out the dough first into a square, placing the butter brick in the centre and folding over the outer dough, pinching together the edges well – rather like completely opening up and closing an envelope. Both ways work equally well.) Fold the pastry strip into three, cover with a cloth wrung out in cold water and leave in a cool place for 15 minutes. Roll out dough into a strip, fold both sides towards the middle, then fold together, rather like closing a book. Cover with a cloth and leave in a cool place for 30 minutes. Roll out into a strip, fold into three

parts as before, leave under a damp cloth for 10 minutes, then roll it out and fold sides towards middle, fold over as before. Leave in a cool place (under a damp cloth) for at least 30 minutes before use.

Bake at 210°C/410°F/Gas 6½ (unless otherwise stated in the recipe), oven pre-heated for 15 to 20 minutes.

The following points are important:

(1) Do not butter and flour the baking sheet — rinse it in cold water and do not wipe it dry.

(2) When cutting the pastry into required shapes, use a hot, wet cutter or knife. The best way to handle this is to stand knife or cutter in a jug of hot water by the side of the pastry board.

(3) When the pastry is 'resting' it must always be covered with a cloth previously wrung out in cold water.

(4) When rolling and folding the pastry, use as little flour on the pastry board as possible and always brush it off the pastry (I do not actually brush, but blow it off — unprofessional, but it works!).

(5) Where the recipe says 'brush top of pastry with egg or milk' be careful that only the top of the pastry is thus treated. Under no circumstances must the liquid run down the sides, as this prevents rising.

(6) Cool away from all draughts — a warm kitchen or in the oven with the heat switched off and the door opened, are the best places.

# Cream Slices

*Cremeschnitten*

Prepare puff pastry as described on page 131. Roll out to about a thickness of 6mm (1/4in), cut into strips about 10cm (4in) wide and bake as described on page 132. When cold cut into 4cm (1 1/2in) slices and sandwich two together with either of the following creams; dust top with icing sugar or cover with thin white water icing.

## Cream Filling I

1/4 litre (1/2 pint) milk
2 egg yolks
Vanilla pod

10g (1/3oz) gelatine
1 tablespoon potato flour
60g (2oz) sugar

Dissolve the gelatine in a little hot water and leave to cool. Blend egg yolks with the potato flour, the sugar and a little cold milk. Heat the remaining milk with vanilla pod and add it gradually to the egg yolks, etc. Whisk over steam until thick, remove from heat and add the dissolved gelatine. Whisk until cool, remove the vanilla pod and chill cream before using.

## Cream Filling II

Vanilla pod
3 egg yolks
75g (2 1/2oz) sugar

1/8 litre (1/4 pint) cream
1/2 teaspoon cornflour

Mix together egg yolks, sugar and cornflour, add the vanilla pod and whisk over steam until thick. Remove from heat and whisk until cool. Whip the cream and fold it into the egg mixture, remove the vanilla pod.

# 'English Bread'

*Englisches Brot*

250g (1/2lb) flour
125g (4oz) sugar
125g (4oz) butter
1 hard-boiled egg yolk
1 egg yolk

Jam
About 1 tablespoon sugar
65g (3oz) currants
65g (3oz) blanched almonds

Sift together flour and sugar. Cut butter into small pieces, crumble into dry ingredients (flour, sugar and hard-boiled egg yolk). Knead to a dough, roll out as thinly as possible, 3mm (1/8in) and bake at 180°C/350°F/Gas 4 until golden brown. Spread with jam while still warm and cut into two equal parts. Leave to cool on a rack. Place one sheet of pastry on top of the other so that the jam is in the centre. Cream egg yolk with about one tablespoon sugar, spread over top of pastry. Sprinkle with blanched almonds cut into strips and with currants and dry in warm oven (150°C/300°F/Gas 2).

# Guglhupf made with Baking Powder

*Guglhupf Mit Backpulver*

*Guglhupf* can be made with yeast (see page 171, also for general remarks about *Guglhupf* forms) and with baking powder. If made with the latter, there are various delectable varieties – it may be a *Gewoehnlicher Backpulver Guglhupf* (an ordinary *Guglhupf* made with baking powder), a *Rahmguglhupf* (*Guglhupf* made with cream or at least top milk), or a *Marmor Guglhupf* (marbled *Guglhupf* where the mixture is divided into two parts and a little grated or melted chocolate is added to one half. *Marmor Guglhupf* can also be made of a yeast mixture). In special cases, and for special occasions – it may even be a *Sacher Guglhupf*, a particularly good mixture made without raisins and almonds, but covered with chocolate icing after baking.

100g (3¹/2oz) butter
140g (5oz) sugar
5 eggs
280g (10oz) flour
2 teaspoons baking powder

4 tablespoons milk
Grated rind of ¹/2 lemon
Blanched almonds
65g (3oz) washed and
  dried raisins

Prepare Guglhupf mould as described on page 171. Cream butter and sugar. Sift together flour and baking powder. Add well-beaten eggs to butter, alternately with flour and milk. Fold in grated lemon rind and the raisins. Bake at 185°C/360°F/Gas 4¹/2 for about 1 hour. Dust with icing sugar while still warm.

# Brandy Rings

## Cognac Ringerl

1 egg yolk
70g (2¹/2oz) sugar
140g (5oz) flour
140g (5oz) butter
140g (5oz) ground almonds or
  walnuts

Rind of 1 lemon
2 tablespoons brandy
Pinch cinnamon
Icing sugar
Brandy

Sift together sugar and flour, add the ground almonds. Crumble butter into dry ingredients, add the egg yolk, brandy, cinnamon and lemon rind and knead to a smooth dough. Chill for 15 minutes. Roll out to about a 6mm (¹/4in) thickness, cut into rings and set them on a buttered and floured baking sheet. Brush the rings with brandy and dust with icing sugar, add a few more drops of brandy so that they are covered wirh a thick layer of sugar moistened with brandy. Bake at 180°C/350°F/Gas 4 until golden brown.

*Austrian* cooking

# *Butter Rings*

*Butter Ringerl*

100g (3¹/2oz) flour
75g (2¹/2oz) butter
¹/2 cup cream
¹/2 tablespoon rum

*Chopped blanched almonds*
*A little granulated sugar*
*Egg for brushing over pastry*

Sift flour on to a pastry board. Cut butter into small lumps. Make a well in the centre of the flour, pour in cream and the rum. Add the butter and work to a smooth dough with a palette knife. Pat into a round and chill for 15 minutes. Roll out to about a 6mm (¹/4in) thickness and cut into rings, using two circular biscuit cutters of different sizes. Set pastry rings on a buttered and floured baking sheet, bake at 190°C/375°F/Gas 5 until pale golden brown (about 15 minutes). Take out of oven, brush with egg, sprinkle with sugar and chopped almonds and return to oven. Switch off the heat and leave biscuits to dry in the oven.

# *Hazel Nut Biscuits*

*Haselnuss Baeckerei*

2 egg whites
75g (3oz) castor sugar

50g (2oz) toasted hazel nuts
(weighed after skins
have been rubbed off)

Place about 70g (2¹/2oz) of hazel nuts on a baking sheet and put in a hot oven (220°C/425°F/Gas 7). Test after a few minutes – the skins should rub off easily. Put hazel nuts in a clean cloth, rub off the skins. Grind hazel nuts.
   Whisk egg whites until stiff, whisk in half the sugar, fold in remaining sugar alternately with the ground hazel nuts. With the aid of a forcing bag pipe small shapes on to a buttered and floured baking sheet. Bake at 150°C/300°F/Gas 2 until lightly tinged with colour.

# *Hazel Nut Sticks*

*Haselnuss Stengerl*

100g (3½oz) butter
125g (4½oz) sugar
2 egg yolks

150g (5½oz) flour
Ground or finely chopped
  hazel nuts

Cream butter and sugar, work in egg yolk and flour. Knead dough on a pastry board, roll out to 3mm (⅛in) thickness. Cut pastry into strips, brush with remaining egg yolk and sprinkle with hazel nuts. Bake on buttered and floured baking sheet until golden brown (190°C/375°F/Gas 5).

# *Florentines*

*Florentiner*

2 egg whites
85g (3oz) grated chocolate

70g (2½oz) icing sugar
140g (5oz) blanched almonds,
  cut into strips

## *Icing*

1 teaspoon butter

50g (2oz) chocolate

Whisk egg whites until stiff. Whisk in half the sugar, fold in remaining sugar carefully, together with the grated chocolate and the blanched almonds. Place small heaps of this mixture on a buttered baking sheet, well apart. Bake at 150°C/300°F/Gas 2 until light brown in colour and dry. Remove from oven, let cool a little, then remove from baking sheet and place upside down on a rack. Melt chocolate, stir in the butter and mix well. When the biscuits are cool, spread with chocolate, mark with a fork. Leave to dry, then arrange on a plate with the chocolate side down.

# *Austrian* cooking

## *Filled Honeycakes*

*Gefuellte Lebkuchen*

125g (4oz) honey
60g (2oz) sugar
1 tablespoon cinnamon
Pinch ground cloves
250g (8oz) flour

1 egg
1/2 teaspoon baking powder
Halved blanched almonds
Egg white for brushing over
  pastry

### Filling

60g (2oz) ground hazel nuts
60g (2oz) sugar

30g (1oz) mixed peel (chopped)
1 egg

Heat honey, then add cinnamon, cloves and sugar. Stir well and leave to
cool. Add flour, previously sifted with the baking powder, and the egg. Knead
well, cover with a cloth and leave overnight. Mix together all ingredients for
the filling. Roll out dough to about 3mm (1/8in) thickness, cut into shapes
and spread half of them with the filling. Place remaining honeycakes over
the ones spread with filling, brush with egg white and decorate with halved
blanched almonds. Bake at gas mark 170°C/345°F/Gas 3½.

# *Gerstnerkrapfen*

2 eggs
50g (2oz) sugar
50g (2oz) flour
15g (1/2oz) melted butter

Glacé fruit
Rum
Raspberry or strawberry jam
Thin white water icing

Heat oven to 230°C/450°F/Gas 8. Place eggs and sugar in a bowl and whisk over steam until thick and fluffy. Remove from heat, whisk until cool, fold in flour and lemon rind, finally fold in melted butter. Turn heat down to 200°C/400°F/Gas 6. Spread mixture to thickness of a finger on a buttered and floured baking sheet and bake until golden brown (about 10 to 15 minutes). Cut into rounds with a pastry cutter while still hot (dip pastry cutter into flour from time to time), remove pastry from baking sheet and set to cool on a sieve. For each round of pastry allow 10g (1/3oz) of glacé fruit, moistened with rum and bound with a little jam. Arrange glacé fruit in centre of each round, cover with thin white water icing and leave to dry.

# *Gleichheitskuchen*

3 eggs and their weight in sugar
Flour and butter

Cherries, redcurrants or
  grapes

Wash and dry the fruit in a sieve. Dust the fruit very lightly with flour. Separate egg yolks and whites. Cream butter and sugar, add egg yolks gradually. Fold in the stiffly beaten egg whites alternately with the flour. The mixture is very stiff indeed.

Spread cake mixture in a buttered and floured cake tin (tradition has it that it should be an oblong one) and place the floured fruit on top, pressing it down very lightly. Bake at 190°C/375°F/Gas 5 (this usually takes just over an hour). Ease the cake a little from the sides of the cake tin and leave in the oven with the heat switched off and the door slightly open for about 15 minutes, then turn the cake carefully on to a sieve and leave it to cool, fruit side uppermost. It is served dusted thickly with vanilla sugar.

# *Austrian* cooking

## *Husarenkrapferl*

70g (2¹/2oz) sugar
140g (5oz) butter
180g (6¹/2oz) flour
1–2 egg yolks

A little grated lemon rind
Jam
Egg for brushing over pastry

Sift together sugar and flour, add grated lemon rind. Crumble butter into dry
ingredients, add the egg yolk and knead to a smooth dough. Pat into a
round and chill for about 20 to 30 minutes. Pinch small lumps off the dough
and roll into balls between the palms of the hands. Set these balls on a
buttered and floured baking sheet. With the handle of a wooden cooking
spoon (dipped into flour from time to time) make a dent in the centre of each
pastry ball – this will spread it a little. Brush pastry with eggwhite - a few
chopped blanched almonds sprinkled over the pastry before baking greatly
enhance the taste – and bake at 185–190°C/365–375°F/Gas 4¹/2–5 until
golden brown. Remove from baking sheet while still warm and put small dab
of jam in the centre of each round. Dust with vanilla sugar.

# *Ischl Tartlets*

### *Ischler Krapfen*

120g (4oz) butter
120g (4oz) flour
60g (2oz) sugar
60g (2oz) ground hazel nuts, walnuts
  or almonds (not blanched)

Raspberry or redcurrant jam
Chocolate icing
A few hazel nuts

Mix together all dry ingredients, crumble butter into these and work to a smooth dough. Pat into a round and chill for at least 30 minutes, longer if possible. Roll out to 3mm (1/8in) thickness, stamp into rounds and bake on buttered and floured baking sheet (190°C/375°F/Gas 5). Remove from baking sheet and cool on a rack. When cold sandwich 2 and 2 together with jam and cover top (not sides) with chocolate icing or melted chocolate. Place a hazel nut in centre of each round. At the famous *Zauner* patisserie in Ischl, where these *Krapfen* originated, and are still served as a *specialité de la maison*, they are always sandwiched together with very good chocolate butter icing.

# *Chestnut Slices*

### *Kastanienschnitten*

Prepare and bake mixture as for *Zigeunerschnitten* (see page 164). Cut into 5cm (2in) wide strips and sprinkle with sherry or brandy. Whip 80ml (1/8 pint) cream until stiff and fold into 175g (6oz) sweetened chestnut purée, add a few drops of Maraschino and spread thickly over the cake base. Sprinkle with some biscuit crumbs and chill while preparing chocolate icing (see page 213). Spread icing carefully over the chestnut cream, chill again, then cut into slices.

Sweetened chestnut purée can be bought in most good food shops. If not available, use cooked and sieved chestnuts beaten to a cream with a little top milk and icing sugar to taste.

# 'Hedgehogs'

*Igel*

For this you need about 7 or 8 small sponge cake rounds – about 5cm (2in) in diameter and 1cm (1/2in) high. Set sponge cakes on a flat dish, sprinkle with a little liqueur or brandy and chill lightly. Cream 60g (2oz) of butter with one tablespoon of sugar. Gradually add one egg yolk, beat mixture well, then add very gradually – almost drop by drop – two tablespoons strong black coffee. Pile a little of the cream on top of each sponge round, spike with toasted blanched almonds cut into strips.

# Children's Teacake 'Children's Rusks'

*Kinderzwieback*

2 eggs
2 tablespoons sugar

2 tablespoons flour
1/4 teaspoon baking powder

Sift together flour and baking powder, sift again. Separate egg yolks and whites. Whisk egg yolks with sugar until thick and creamy. Whip egg whites until stiff. Fold egg whites into egg yolks, alternately with the flour. Bake in a buttered and floured oblong cake tin (170°C/325°F/Gas 3). Remove from tin while still hot and cool on a rack. Next day cut into 6mm (1/4in) slices and toast in oven on both sides. Serve sprinkled with vanilla sugar.

# Crescents

*Kipferl aus Zuckerteig*

60g (2oz) butter
120g (4oz) flour
1 egg yolk

1 teaspoon lemon juice
45g (1½oz) sugar

Sift together flour and sugar, crumble butter into the dry ingredients and knead to a smooth dough with the egg yolk and lemon juice. Roll small pieces of the dough between the palms of the hands, shape into crescents or letters of the alphabet. Bake on a buttered and floured sheet (185°C/360°F/Gas 4½) until golden brown. Dust with icing sugar while still hot.

# Linzer Slices

*Linzerschnitten*

## Pastry

250g (9oz) flour
200g (7oz) butter
250g (9oz) sugar

1 egg yolk
A little lemon juice and rind

## Filling

140ml (¼ pint) cream
40g (1½oz) sugar

50g (2oz) grated chocolate

Sift together flour and sugar, crumble butter into this. Knead to a smooth dough with the egg yolk and lemon juice and rind. Roll out to 6mm (¼in) thickness, bake on buttered and floured baking sheet at 190°C/375°F/Gas 5. Cut into slices while still warm. Whip cream until stiff, whisk in the sugar. Set aside a little of the whipped cream for decoration. Fold grated chocolate into remaining cream and spread half the pastry slices with this. Top with remaining slices and decorate with small blobs of whipped cream. Dust icing sugar over the top.

# *Austrian* cooking

## *Almond 'Bread'*

*Mandelbrot*

260g (10oz) flour
125g (4¹/₂oz) butter
100g (3¹/₂oz) chopped blanched
  almonds

75g (3oz) sugar
1 egg yolk
A little milk

Crumble butter into dry ingredients, add egg yolk and sufficient milk to make a stiff dough. Knead until smooth. Shape into a roll and chill well, preferably overnight. Cut into thin slices and bake on buttered and floured baking sheet until golden brown on one side (190°C/375°F/Gas 5), turn carefully, return to oven, switch off heat and finish drying in oven.

The pastry can be kept for quite a long time in the refrigerator before baking.

## *Almond Slices*

*Mandelschnitten*

45g (1¹/₂oz) sugar
90g (3oz) butter
125g (4¹/₂oz) flour
3 egg whites
120g (4oz) granulated sugar

90g (3oz) chopped almonds
¹/₂ teaspoon flour
Jam
Melted chocolate

Cream butter and sugar, add flour and work to a dough. Line a buttered baking sheet with this pastry (about 3mm (¹/₈in) deep) and bake at 180°C/350°F/Gas 4 until top is lightly set (about 5 minutes). Meanwhile whisk egg whites until stiff, add sugar and almonds and stir over lowest possible heat in a thick saucepan until mixture is light pink. Remove from heat, stir in half teaspoon flour. Spread half-baked pastry with jam and then with the almond paste. Return pastry to oven (200°C/400°F/Gas 6) until golden brown. Cut into squares while still hot, carefully dip one side into melted chocolate and set on waxed paper to dry.

# *Almond Kisses*

*Mandel Busserl*

Mix 85g (3oz) of blanched and finely ground almonds with 170g (6oz) of icing sugar. Care must be taken that almonds are perfectly dry before being ground and it is best to spread them on a flat dish after blanching to dry thoroughly. Gradually add a little egg white and one teaspoon lemon juice, beating all the time with a wooden spoon. Quantity of egg white required varies according to the size of the egg, but one medium-sized egg white is about sufficient for the above recipe. The mixture must not be wet but it should be 'workable'. Begin creaming the mixture as soon as this stage has been reached and continue creaming until the mixture is light and fluffy. Cover with a sieve and leave to stand for several hours – overnight if possible. Pipe small rounds of this mixture on to a very lightly buttered and floured baking sheet, leave to dry for 1 hour and bake at 150°C/300°F/Gas 2 (pre-heated oven) until lightly tinged with colour.

# *Austrian* cooking

## *Cherry Strudel*

*Kirschenstrudel*

*Strudel pastry as described on page 159*

### *Filling*

500g (1lb) Morello cherries
3/4 cup sugar
1 1/2 cups breadcrumbs
Butter for frying

Melted butter
Chopped walnuts
Apricot jam

Prepare Strudel pastry as described on page 159. Stone the cherries and sprinkle them with sugar. Fry breadcrumbs in butter. Sprinkle the fried breadcrumbs evenly over the pastry, then sprinkle cherries and chopped walnuts over half the surface only. Sprinkle with melted butter and dot with a little apricot jam. Tear off the rather thick rim which overhangs the table and start rolling the strudel by lifting the cloth at the 'cherry' end. Roll up very carefully, like a Swiss roll, close up ends and place on buttered baking sheet, forming a horseshoe. Brush with melted butter and cover with greaseproof paper. Bake in a moderate oven (180–185°C/350–360°F/Gas 4–41/2) for about 45 minutes, removing paper towards the end. Sprinkle with vanilla sugar.

# *Honey Biscuits*

*Lebzelt Baekerei*

200g (7oz) sugar
2 eggs
Pinch each powdered
  cinnamon, cloves, nutmeg
  and ginger

170g (6oz) honey
500g (17oz) flour
1/2 teaspoon bicarbonate
  of soda
Egg for brushing over pastry

Sift together bicarbonate of soda and flour. Put sugar and eggs in a bowl and whisk until light and frothy. Add the warmed honey, spices and finally the flour. Mix well with a wooden spoon, pat into a round, cover and chill for 3 hours. After that time knead a little, then roll out the dough to about 6mm (1/4in) thickness. Cut into shapes with a biscuit cutter. Brush with egg and bake for about 7 minutes on a well-buttered and floured baking sheet (200°C/400°F/Gas 6). These biscuits harden slightly as they cool and soften again during storage.

*Austrian* cooking

# *Apricot Strudel*

*Marillenstrudel*

250g (1/2lb) puff pastry (see
   page 132)
Apricot jam

Apricots
Sugar
Egg for brushing over pastry

Roll out pastry and trim into a rectangle measuring about 25cm x 15cm (10in x 6in). Cut off two 1cm (1/2in) strips so that pastry now measures 25cm x 12.5cm (10in x 5in). Spread a little warmed apricot jam down centre of pastry to within 3.5cm (1 1/2in) of either edge. Cover centre strip with halved stoned apricots, sprinkle with sugar. Brush the uncovered side strips with egg, being careful that egg does not run down the cut edge. Fold one side of pastry over apricots, brush with egg fold over other side. Make small strips from cut-off pieces of pastry and lay across fold. Secure ends. Brush over top of Strudel – but not over any of the cut edges – with egg. Set Strudel on a damped baking sheet. Light the oven at 220°C/425°F/Gas 7 and heat it for 15 minutes before putting in Strudel. This gives the pastry time to 'settle' on the baking sheet. Bake until golden brown, lowering heat to 200°C/400°F/Gas 6 after about 20 minutes. When the Strudel is baked, dust it with icing sugar and return it to the oven for a few minutes with the heat switched off.

# *Guglhupf Made with Cream*

*Rahmguglhupf*

Prepare a *Guglhupf* mould as described on page 171. Separate yolks and whites of three eggs. Sift together 270g (9 1/2oz) of flour with a teaspoon baking powder, sift again. Whisk egg yolks with 90g (3oz) of sugar, gradually add 1/4 litre (1/2 pint) cream and continue whisking until well blended and fluffy. Whisk egg whites until stiff, fold in two tablespoons sugar and whisk until smooth. Fold flour into egg yolks, etc., alternately with the stiffly beaten whites. Add a little grated lemon rind and about half a cup of washed and dried raisins. Bake for about 45 minutes at 185°C/360°F/Gas 4 1/2. Dust with vanilla sugar while still warm.

# Sour Cream Strudel

*Milchrahmstrudel*

Strudel pastry (see page 159)

## Filling

100g (3¹/2oz) butter
100g (3¹/2oz) sugar
4 eggs
¹/4 litre (¹/2 pint) sour cream
120g (4¹/2oz) breadcrumbs

Melted butter
420ml (³/4 pint) milk
Grated lemon rind
75g (3oz) raisins

Prepare Strudel pastry as described on page 159. Wash and dry the raisins, separate egg yolks and whites. Cream butter and sugar, add the egg yolks and lemon rind. Fold in the stiffly beaten egg whites alternately with the sour cream. Spread this filling over half the pastry, sprinkle with raisins and breadcrumbs. Brush the other half of the pastry with melted butter. Tear off the thick rim of pastry which overhangs the table. Roll up Strudel by lifting tablecloth at the filled end and roll as for Swiss roll. Set Strudel in a buttered deep baking dish, shaping the pastry into a 'snail'. Brush with melted butter.

Bake at 185°C/360°F/Gas 4¹/2 until pastry begins to brown, pour the hot milk over it, turn up the heat to 190°C/375°F/Gas 5 and finish off baking. Serve with *Kanarienmilch* (see page 101).

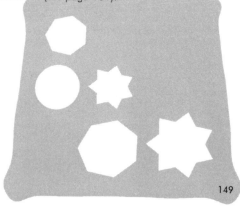

# *Austrian* cooking

# *Pastry Slices*

*Muerbe Schnitten*

150g (5½oz) butter
150g (5½oz) flour
80g (3oz) sugar

1 egg
½ teaspoon baking powder

## *Filling*

100g (3½oz) ground walnuts,
  hazelnuts or almonds
100g (3½oz) sugar

2 tablespoons milk
Breadcrumbs

Sift together flour, sugar and baking powder. Add the egg and the butter and work to a smooth dough. Roll two-thirds of the dough into a strip about 6mm (¼in) thick. Set on a buttered and floured baking sheet and bake for about 8 minutes at 190°C/375°F/Gas 5. Meanwhile mix together ground walnuts, etc., sugar and milk and, if necessary, sufficient breadcrumbs to give a smooth spreading consistency. A few drops of rum improve the flavour. Roll remaining pastry into strips. Take half-baked pastry from the oven, spread with the nut mixture, arrange uncooked pastry strips in a criss-cross pattern over the filling and return to oven to complete baking. Serve cold, cut into slices and sprinkled thickly with vanilla sugar.

# Nut Roll

*Nuss Roulade*

125g (4oz) ground almonds,
  walnuts or hazel nuts
3 eggs

Fine breadcrumbs or
  cake crumbs
90g (3½oz) icing sugar

Whisk egg yolks with sugar until pale and creamy. Fold in ground nuts alternately with the stiffly beaten egg whites. Spread on a baking sheet previously buttered and spread with fine breadcrumbs or cakecrumbs. Bake for about a 15 minutes at 180°C/350°F/Gas 4. Remove carefully and roll lightly over sugared paper. When cold unroll carefully and fill, roll up again. The traditional filling is sweetened whipped cream into which small wild strawberries and a dash of Kirsch have been folded. I have on occasion used the cream filling described on page 206 (see Nut Gateau) and strawberries and ice-cream, though very unorthodox, taste exceedingly good as a filling.

*Austrian* cooking

# Nut Boats

*Nuss Schipperl*

70g (2oz) icing sugar
140g (4oz) butter

210g (6oz) flour

## Filling

60g (2oz) ground nuts (walnuts
  or hazel nuts)
60g (2oz) icing sugar
A few drops rum
A little grated lemon or orange
  rind and juice

2 tablespoons lightly toasted
  biscuit crumbs or cake crumbs
A little milk
Water icing

Crumble butter into flour and sugar and work to a smooth dough. Pat into a round and chill for 30 minutes. Roll out pastry and line small patty tins with it. Bake 'blind' at 190°C/375°F/Gas 5.

Mix together all ingredients for the filling and add sufficient milk to make a stiff paste. Fill pastry shells, smooth top with a knife dipped into hot water and cover with thin water icing.

# Jam Envelopes

*Polsterzipfel*

Cream cheese pastry
  (see page 161)

Jam
Egg for brushing over pastry

Roll out pastry to 3mm (⅛in) thickness, cut into 5cm (2in) squares (a zig-zag cutting wheel gives a nice finish). Place a blob of jam in the centre, fold over and press down edges so that pastry forms a triangle. Brush with egg and bake until golden brown (195°C/385°F/Gas 5½). Sprinkle with vanilla sugar before serving.

In some parts of Austria this is also known as *Hasenohren* (Hare's ears).

# 'Saddle of Venison Gateau'

*Rehruecken*

This is simply a good chocolate cake baked in a special cake tin, then covered with chocolate icing and spiked with strips of blanched almonds to imitate the larding on a saddle of venison (the literal translation of *Rehruecken*). The special cake tin is oblong and fluted in a particular way to denote the slices into which the cake is cut later on. It also has a 'dent' running down the centre, and after the cake has been covered with chocolate icing this dent is sometimes studded with halved glacé cherries or filled with redcurrant jelly to denote the 'backbone'. The cake can, of course, be baked in an ordinary cake tin and a good helping of sweetened whipped cream with each slice is optional. The recipe given below is for a very moist *Rehruecken*, but any good chocolate cake mixture can be used – *Weiche Schokoladetorte*, or *Schokoladetorte mit Mandeln* (see pages 219 and 216) or even *Sachertorte* (see page 214) when the cake becomes known as *Sacher Rehruecken*.

125g (4½oz) butter
110g (4oz) chocolate
3 rounded tablespoons icing
  sugar
45g (1½oz) good breadcrumbs

4 eggs
Powdered cinnamon and
  powdered cloves
Rum

Separate egg yolks and whites. Break chocolate into small pieces and set in a warm place to melt. Cream butter and sugar, gradually add the melted (but not hot) chocolate and the egg yolks. Stir in a dash of rum. Fold in stiffly beaten egg whites alternately with the breadcrumbs, cloves and cinnamon. Bake in buttered and floured oblong cake tin (185°C/360°F/Gas 4½). When cold spread with warmed redcurrant jelly, cover with chocolate icing (see page 213) and spike with strips of blanched almonds.

# *Austrian* cooking

# *Rose cakes*

*Rosenkrapfen*

Deep fat for frying
140g (5oz) flour
45g (1½oz) butter
2 egg yolks
1 tablespoon top milk

1 tablespoon brandy, rum or
 sherry
30g (1oz) icing sugar
Pinch salt, jam and a little egg
 white

Sift together salt, flour and sugar, sift again on to a board. Make a well in
the centre, pour in the egg yolks, top milk and the brandy and work to a stiff
paste with the butter. Cover with a cloth and leave for 15 minutes. Roll out
as thin as possible. Have ready three round pastry cutters, graded in size,
and cut out an equal number of rounds in each size.

   Place the two smaller rounds on top of the largest round moistening the
centre with a little egg white. Press down the centre of each 'rose' with a
fingertip to make a small well. Make a few incisions round each rose to mark
the petals. Have ready a small pan of smoking-hot fat and drop in the roses
separately, petal side down. Turn when one side has browned fry on other
side. Drain on kitchen paper, then dust with vanilla sugar. Place a small blob
of jam in centre of each 'rose'.

# *Redcurrant Flan*

*Ribisel Kuchen*

Prepare a pastry with 60g (2oz) of sugar, 120g (4oz) of butter and 180g
(6oz) of flour, a few drops of lemon juice and line a buttered and floured
rectangular flan tin with this. Bake blind. When baked, but still hot, cover
thickly with redcurrants, sprinkle with a little sugar. Whisk two egg whites
until stiff, whisk in 50g (2oz) of caster sugar. Pile whipped egg white over
redcurrants and bake in cool oven until meringue top has set
(130°C/250°F/Gas 1). Cut into slices when cool.

# Guglhupf à la Sacher

*Sacher Guglhupf*

| | |
|---|---|
| 140g (5oz) butter | 2 tablespoons rum |
| 3 egg yolks | 1 teaspoon baking powder |
| 1 egg | 280g (10oz) flour |
| 140g (5oz) icing sugar | Jam |
| About 5 tablespoons milk | Chocolate icing (see page 213) |

Butter a *Guglhupf* mould, sprinkle with flour, but do not cover with almonds as for other types of *Guglhupf*. Cream butter well, add the egg yolks and the whole egg alternately with the sugar. Beat well, then add the milk, rum and the flour (previously sifted with the baking powder). Bake for about 45 minutes at 185°C/360°F/Gas 4½. When cold brush lightly with melted jam, then cover with chocolate icing (see page 213).

# Chocolate Kisses

*Schokolade Busserl*

| | |
|---|---|
| 2 egg whites | 140g (5oz) blanched almonds |
| 70g (2½oz) icing sugar | Rice paper |
| 85g (3oz) softened chocolate | |

Cut almonds into strips. Whip egg whites until stiff, fold in half of the icing sugar, whisk again until smooth. Fold in remaining sugar, softened chocolate (which must not be hot) and almonds. Drop in spoonfuls on to rounds of rice paper, leaving room to spread. Bake in very slow oven (130–140°C/250–275°/ Gas 1–2) until set and dry.

# *Chocolate Fondant Biscuits*

*Schokolade Fondant*

200g (7oz) sugar
140g (5oz) butter
140g (5oz) plain chocolate

140g (5oz) ground toasted almonds
 (not blanched)
1 tablespoon flour
Glacé cherries for decoration

Break chocolate into small pieces and set to soften in a warm place. Cream butter and sugar, add flour, almonds and the softened chocolate.

Arrange small 'dabs' of the mixture on a buttered and floured baking sheet, well apart. Flatten a little with a knife and decorate with halved glacé cherries. Bake at 200°C/400°F/Gas 6. Remove carefully from paper while still hot.

# *Chocolate Slices*

*Schokoladeschnitten*

Cream 80g (3oz) of butter with 80g (3oz) of sugar. Add four egg yolks gradually, as well as 80g (3oz) of grated chocolate. Fold in stiffly beaten whites of five eggs alternately with 50g (2 scant oz) of fine breadcrumbs and one teaspoon grated lemon rind. Spread about 3.5cm (1½in) high in a buttered and floured rectangular cake tin and bake at 185°C/360°F/ Gas 4½. Remove from tin while still warm, cool and cut into slices. Cut slices through once and fill with chocolate cream as for *Panamatorte* (see page 209) or *Dobos Torte* (see page 196). Spread a little of the cream over the top as well and sprinkle with chocolate vermicelli or grated chocolate.

# 'Chocolate Sausage'

*Schokoladewurst*

120g (4oz) icing sugar
1 egg
120g (4oz) ground almonds
  (blanched)

100g (3oz) grated chocolate
40g (1 generous oz) chopped mixed peel
40g (1 generous oz) blanched almonds
  cut into strips

Cream egg and sugar, add other ingredients. Shape into a thick roll and dry very slowly in oven ('after baking' heat is sufficient and the drying may be done in stages). Cut after 3 days.

# 'Rascals'

*Spitzbuben*

50g (2oz) sugar
105g (3¹/₂oz) butter
1 egg

140g (5oz) flour
Jam

Sift together flour and sugar. Work to a smooth dough with the butter and the egg. Roll out on a floured pastry board as thin as possible and cut into shapes with a biscuit cutter. Bake at 190°C/375°F/Gas 5 on a buttered and floured baking sheet until golden brown. Remove from baking sheet while still hot, sandwich two and two together with jam when lightly cooled.

# *Chocolate Roll*

*Schokolade Roulade*

50g (2oz) chocolate
3 eggs
50g (2oz) sugar

25g (1oz) ground almonds (not blanched)
Sweetened whipped cream

Break chocolate into small pieces and put in a warm place to soften. Add egg yolks and sugar and whisk until thick and fluffy. Fold in stiffly beaten egg whites, finally fold in ground almonds. Spread on a Swiss roll tin, lined with buttered greaseproof paper and bake (190°C/375°F/Gas 5). Turn out on to sugared paper, remove paper sticking to pastry. Roll up lightly over sugared paper. When cold unroll, spread with sweetened whipped cream and roll up again. Dust with icing sugar.

# *Cornets*

*Stanitzl*

2 eggs                3/4 cup flour                3/4 cup sugar

Whisk eggs with sugar until thick and fluffy. Fold in sifted flour. Drop in spoonfuls on to a well-buttered and floured baking sheet, leaving space for each round to spread. Flatten a little with a palette knife. Bake at 180°C/350°F/Gas 4 until pale golden brown. Remove from baking sheet while still hot and quickly twist into cornets (roll round the handle of a wooden cooking spoon and set cornets in a glass to keep the shape). The pastry hardens as it cools. Ideally they should be filled with sugared wild strawberries and cream, but sugared garden strawberries and a spoonful of good vanilla ice-cream are quite delicious too. For a more luxurious pastry, replace part of the flour with ground almonds or walnuts.

# Cakes, Pastries and Biscuits

# *Strudel Paste*

*Strudelteig*

There are *Strudeln* and *Strudeln*. Baked and boiled. Made with puff pastry and made with yeast. Savoury and sweet. But when the talk is of *Strudelteig* (the paste) it always means one thing only – a recipe of the type quoted below. Sometimes it may contain an egg, sometimes the egg yolk or the white only.

Strudel paste is not difficult to make. It requires a little practice, a 'feeling' for the paste as it were, and you are bound to get a few tears and holes now and then. Everybody does. In such cases I usually blame the flour, mumbling something about the necessity of *glattes Mehl*, which is, of course, quite true. *Strudel* paste should be made with what is known in Austria as *glattes* flour. But it *can* be made – and I have made it many times – with ordinary plain flour.

## The Pastry

250g (8oz) plain flour
1 teaspoon vinegar or
  lemon juice
1 heaped teaspoon butter

About 140ml (1/4 pint) warm water
Pinch salt
Melted butter

Have everything nicely warmed – hands, liquid, pastry board. A wooden pastry board is much preferable to an enamelled one. If you have to use the latter, wipe it over with a cloth wrung out in hot water before starting. Sift flour and salt on to clean pastry board. Make a well in the centre, pour in vinegar or lemon juice. Cut butter into flour or crumble it with your fingers. Add enough warm water to make a soft dough and knead well until it 'blisters'. Bring it down on to the pastry board with a few smart slaps from time to time. Sprinkle dough with flour and cover with a warmed bowl – do not let the bowl touch the dough. Leave in a warm place for 30 minutes, renewing the covering bowl should it cool too rapidly. Prepare the filling during this time and set it aside. After 30 minutes the dough should be 'ripe' to start pulling operations. Cover a kitchen table with a clean cloth and sprinkle it with flour. If the kitchen table is not large enough, use the dining table (if larger) or halve the dough before you start pulling. Place the dough – floured side down – on the cloth and carefully roll out as far as it will go. Brush with a little melted butter, then slip your hands underneath the dough

159

and pull it, using the balls of your thumbs, not the fingers, and always working from the middle, being careful not to tear the dough.

When the dough is pulled out to paper thinness, brush the pastry again with melted butter and leave to dry for 10 to 15 minutes.

# Biscuits I

*Teebaekerei I*

120g (4oz) butter
180g (6oz) flour
180g (6oz) sugar
180g (6oz) ground almonds
  (unblanched)
30g (1oz) grated chocolate
1 egg or 2 egg yolks

Pinch cinnamon
Pinch nutmeg
Egg white for brushing over
  pastry
Ground almonds for sprinkling
  over pastry

Mix together the dry ingredients, cut butter into small pieces and crumble into dry ingredients. Work to a dough with the egg. Knead until quite smooth, roll out to 3mm (1/8in) thickness. Cut into shapes with a biscuit cutter, set on a floured buttered baking sheet, brush with egg white and sprinkle with ground almonds. Bake at 190°C/375°F/Gas 5 until nicely browned.

# Biscuits II

*Teebaekerei II*

280g (10oz) flour
70g (2½oz) butter
100g (3½oz) sugar
1 egg

About 3 tablespoons cream
  or sour milk
A pinch baking powder

Sift together dry ingredients, crumble butter into the mixture and work to a smooth dough with the egg and the cream or sour milk. Knead well, roll out on a floured pastry board and leave night overnight in a cool place. Cut into shapes with a biscuit cutter and bake until golden brown (190°C/375°F/Gas 5).

# Cream Cheese Slices

*Topfenschnitten*

1 egg
25g (1oz) sugar

### Cream

50g (2oz) butter
50g (2oz ) sugar
1 egg yolk

25g (1oz) ground walnuts or
  almonds
1 teaspoon flour

1 teaspoon grated lemon rind
About 75g (2½oz) cream cheese
Toasted ground almonds

Whisk together egg and sugar over steam until thick, remove from heat and whisk until cool. Fold in ground walnuts or almonds and flour. Spread on a buttered and floured baking sheet and bake at 195°C/385°F/Gas 5½. Cut into slices and remove from baking sheet while still hot.

Cream butter and sugar, add the egg yolk and the cream cheese, beat in the grated lemon rind. Spread this cream thickly over the pastry and sprinkle toasted ground almonds over the top.

# Puff Pastry made with Cream Cheese

*Topfenblaetterteig*

125g (4oz) flour
125g (4oz) butter

125g (4oz) cream cheese

Sift flour on to pastry board. Cut butter into small pieces, crumble cream cheese and butter into flour, handling dough as lightly as possible. Pat dough into a round and chill well before using as required (chill overnight if possible). You can also use it for sausage rolls or – cut into strips, brushed with egg white, sprinkled with coarse salt, paprika and caraway seeds and baked – as a cocktail savoury. An egg yolk may be added to the basic recipe quoted above.

# Cream Cheese Cresents

*Topfenkipferl*

Pastry as before.

## Filling

80g (3oz) blanched almonds
2 egg whites
Juice and rind 1/2 lemon

30g (1oz) sugar
Egg yolk for brushing over
   pastry

Grate almonds finely. Whip egg whites until stiff, whisk in the sugar. Fold in almonds, lemon juice and rind. Roll out pastry to 3mm (1/8in) thickness, cut into squares. Place a little of the filling in the centre of each square, fold over pastry, roll up and shape into a crescent. Brush with egg yolk and bake until golden brown (190°C/375°F/Gas 5).

# Vanilla Cresents

*Vanillekipferl*

30g (1oz) ground almonds
   (unblanched)
60g (2oz) sugar

90g (3oz) butter
120g (4oz) flour
Vanilla sugar

Sift together flour and sugar. Add ground almonds. Cut butter into small pieces and crumble into dry ingredients. Knead into a firm paste. Take small pieces of the dough, roll between your hands, bend into crescents. Bake on a buttered and floured baking sheet at 190°C/375°F/Gas 5 until dark golden brown. Roll in vanilla sugar (icing sugar in which a vanilla pod has been kept) while still hot.

# *Zaunerstollen*

These should really be made with *Zauner Oblaten* (wafers made specially by the House of Zauner in Ischl), but ordinary ice wafers can be used, provided they are dry and not soggy.

*125ml (1/4 pint) cream*
*100g (3oz) grated chocolate*
*Chocolate icing (see page 213)*

*100g (3oz) hazel nuts*
*100g (3oz) ice wafers*

Place hazel nuts on a baking sheet and put them in a hot oven for a few minutes until skins come off easily. Put hazel nuts in a clean towel, rub off skins and then grind hazel nuts, or chop them finely. Put chocolate in a saucepan together with the cream and bring slowly to the boil, stirring constantly. Remove from heat, whisk until cool. Add hazel nuts and crumbled ice wafers. Pour into an oblong cake tin lined with buttered greaseproof paper and leave in a cold place until well set. Turn out of mould, remove paper and ice with chocolate icing. Cut with a hot knife. (It is best left for a day or even two before cutting.)

# *Morello Cherry Cake*

*Weichselkuchen*

*60g (2oz) butter*
*60g (2oz) sugar*
*60g (2oz) ground almonds*
  *(unblanched)*
*30g (1oz) fine breadcrumbs*

*2 eggs*
*A little lemon juice*
*A pinch cinnamon and*
  *nutmeg*
*1 cup stoned morello cherries*

Separate egg yolks and whites. Cream butter with half the sugar, add yolks gradually. Whisk egg whites until stiff, whisk in remaining sugar. Fold stiffly beaten egg whites into creamed butter, alternately with ground almonds and breadcrumbs. Fold in morello cherries, lemon juice, cinnamon and nutmeg. Bake in a buttered and floured cake tin at 180°C/350°F/Gas 4 for about 35 minutes.

# Widow's Kisses

*Witwenkuesse*

2 egg whites
70g (2¹/₂oz) sugar
70g (2¹/₂oz) chopped nuts

35g (1¹/₂oz) chopped mixed peel
Rice paper

Whisk egg whites and sugar over steam until thick, remove from heat, whisk until cold. Fold in chopped nuts (walnuts, hazel nuts or almonds or a mixture of all three), chopped mixed peel. Arrange in small heaps on rounds of rice paper and bake at 100°C/200°F/Gas ¹/₂ until lightly tinged with colour.

# Gipsy Slices

*Zigeunerschnitten*

These are filled with the most luscious of all cream fillings, *Pariser Creme*. Cream is an absolute necessity and it's no good trying any substitute. It just doesn't work.

2 eggs
50g (2 scant oz) granulated sugar
60g (2oz) flour

30g (1oz) chocolate
20g (generous ¹/₂oz) butter

Break chocolate into small pieces, place in a bowl, together with the butter and set to soften in a warm place. Put eggs and sugar in a bowl and whisk over steam until thick, remove from fire and whisk until cool. Lightly fold in flour and finally the softened butter and chocolate. Spread about 1cm (¹/₂in) thick on buttered greaseproof paper, place on a baking sheet and bake at 200°C/400°F/Gas 6. Remove paper while still hot. Cut into slices, cut through each slice once and fill with:

## Cakes, Pastries and Biscuits

### Pariser Creme

140ml (1/4 pint) cream          60g (2oz) grated chocolate

Put grated chocolate in a thick saucepan, add cream and bring to boil slowly, stirring constantly. Leave to rise once, remove from heat and stir until cool. Chill well. Whisk lightly, until it will just hold its shape. Chill again before using.

# Cinnamon Stars

*Zimtsterne*

250g (9oz) sugar
250g (9oz) blanched almonds
  (ground)
1 teaspoon cinnamon

3 tablespoons water
1/2 egg white
100g (3 1/2oz) icing sugar
Lemon juice

Sift together sugar and cinnamon. Add ground almonds and mix together. Make a little well in centre and add the water and a little egg white (about half an egg white). Knead well to a firm dough. Roll out on a sugared (not floured) pastry board to 6mm (1/4in) thickness and cut into stars with a pastry cutter. Place on a sugared pastry sheet and dry at lowest possible heat in oven (heat after oven has been turned off is sufficient), then bake at 150°C/300°F/Gas 2 until deep golden brown. Mix the icing sugar with sufficient lemon juice to give a thick consistency and spread over stars. Leave to dry.

# *Austrian* cooking

## Cheese Biscuits

*Kaesebaekerei*

130g (4¹/₂oz) grated cheese
60g (2oz) butter
130g (4¹/₂oz) flour

1 egg yolk
A few walnuts or hazel nuts
  for decoration

Work all the ingredients to a stiff paste, roll out and cut into shapes. Brush
with a little egg white or milk and place a nut in centre of each biscuit. Bake
until golden brown (190°C/375°F/Gas 5). Alternately, only decorate half
the biscuits with nuts and when cool, sandwich 2 and 2 together with a
paste made of creamed butter to which 1 or 2 finely scraped anchovies
have been added.

## Ham Biscuits

*Schinkenbaeckerei*

Sift together 300g (11oz) of flour with a pinch salt. Crumble 200g (7oz) of
butter into the flour, add two hard-boiled egg yolks and enough cream to
give a stiff paste, about 70ml (3fl oz). Knead well, pat into a round and chill
for 1 hour. Roll out to 3mm (¹/₈in) thickness, brush with egg or egg yolk,
sprinkle with chopped ham. Fold sides to middle, roll out pastry as before.
Brush again with egg, sprinkle again with chopped ham, fold sides to middle
and roll out. Leave for 20 minutes. Roll out to 3mm (¹/₈in) thickness, brush
with egg, sprinkle with coarse salt and caraway seeds and leave for 1 to 2
hours. Cut into strips or shapes and bake in hot oven until golden brown
(200°C/400°F/Gas 6).

# Yeast

There is nothing complicated about cooking with yeast. Recipes may vary, but the basic fundamentals remain the same: A warm, slightly steamy kitchen, as free of draughts as possible. A comfortably warm place for the dough to rise in. Yeast dies if the heat is too great and, failing all else, set the bowl over steam. The necessity of 'proving' the yeast: It is mixed with a little sugar, flour and tepid milk and set in a warm place. This is done for two reasons. Firstly to prove that the yeast is still 'live' – it will come up in a froth of small bubbles if this is the case. If it doesn't, you will not have wasted your other ingredients. Secondly, yeast thus dissolved is more evenly distributed throughout the dough.

Yeast dough is quite tough, though it feels very soft to the touch. It does not require extra-special handling, but it is grateful for being worked on a wooden pastry board. Although the quantities for milk are stated, these vary sometimes, according to the flour.

# *Austrian* cooking

## *Buchteln*

400g (14oz) flour
Pinch salt
About 1/4 litre (8fl oz) milk
3 egg yolks (or 1 egg and
  1 egg yolk)
50g (2oz) sugar

100g (3 1/2oz) butter
Jam
Melted butter for
  brushing over buns
15g (1/2oz) yeast
Grated lemon rind

Set the 90g (3 1/2oz) butter to melt in a warm place. Cream yeast with a
teaspoon of the sugar and a pinch of flour. Heat milk a little, it should only
be tepid. Stir about half of the milk into the creamed yeast and set to prove
in a warm place. Sift flour and salt into a warmed mixing bowl. Put egg yolks
(or egg and egg yolk), remaining sugar, milk and melted butter in a bowl
and whisk until well blended. Make a well in centre of flour and stir egg,
milk, etc., into flour, add lemon rind and yeast. Beat well with a wooden
spoon until dough leaves sides of spoon and bowl clean. Dust with a little
flour and cover with a cloth. Leave to rise for about 1 hour. Butter and lightly
flour a cake tin or deep baking dish. Roll out pastry to about 6mm (1/4 in)
on a floured pastry board and cut into 6cm (2 1/2in) squares. Place a good
dab of jam in centre of each square and fold together (this is best done by
picking up the four corners, pinching them well together in the middle so
that the jam is completely enclosed).

Pack the small buns next to each other – they should touch closely – in
the cake tin after brushing each bun carefully with melted butter. (The
'pinched-together' edges should be at the bottom of the tin.) One good way
of moistening the buns with melted butter is to dip them very lightly into the
melted butter and then spread the butter lightly all over the bun. Brush a little
melted butter over the top of the buns, cover tin with a cloth and leave to
rise for 30 minutes. Bake at 190°C/375°F/Gas 5 until nicely browned. Take
out of cake tin and leave to cool on a wire rack. Separate buns when cold
and sprinkle liberally with icing sugar.

# Carnival Doughnuts

*Faschingskrapfen*

About 80ml (3 scant fl oz) cream
225g (8oz) flour
10g (1/2oz) yeast
1 teaspoon sugar
1 dessertspoon rum
1 teaspoon lemon juice
1 teaspoon orange juice
Fat for frying

1 teaspoon grated orange or
  lemon rind
25g (1oz) sugar
Pinch salt
3 egg yolks
50g (2oz) melted butter
Apricot jam

Respectable *Faschingskrapfen* are noted for the white band which runs right round their plump middles. Apart from that, they should be deep golden brown, nicely rounded and rather well-proportioned. Here then are my own special hints, and it might be as well to say at this point that many a *Krapfen* which lacked some or all of the above qualifications was devoured with prodigious speed in my kitchen!

(1) Have everything nicely warmed – flour, mixing bowl pastry board, hands, etc. – and be careful to shut out all draughts. This is more important with doughnuts than with any other type of yeast pastry.

(2) You may prefer to let dough rise only once, i.e., when the *Krapfen* are already cut out, rather than letting it rise twice, i.e., before rolling it out and then when the doughnuts have been stamped into rounds. Personally I prefer the latter method. It is of course a matter of personal preference, but if you decide to let the *Krapfen* rise only once you must allow more time for this.

(3) Do not expect the dough to be firm – it should be very soft indeed and only just manageable. Press it out with your knuckles rather than rolling it and you will at the same time dispel any small air bubbles which would swell with the frying and spoil the appearance of the finished product. Some cooks even advise a few smart slaps with the hand against the dough for that reason – for which I have so far lacked the courage, though it sounds reasonable enough.

(4) Whenever you handle the doughnuts or the dough itself, turn them upside down, e.g., when you set the doughnuts on the tray to rise, when you put them in the hot fat, etc.

(5) Brush off all flour before putting doughnuts in the fat.

169

(6) In Vienna one could buy special *Krapfenschmalz* to fry doughnuts in. Pure lard (the emphasis is on pure) is best after that, though it does brown the doughnuts rather fast, or really good quality cooking fat. A small piece of beeswax added to either improves the appearance.

(7) Whether rolling out the dough or 'pressing it out' with your knuckles, lift dough very carefully from time to time so that it 'runs' towards the centre – this gives a better shape to the finished product.

(8) Do not cut the *Krapfen* too small – about 6cm (2½in) across is best.

(9) The doughnuts should literally 'swim' in the fat, which means not only that the fat must be deep enough, about 5cm (2in) but also that the *Krapfen* must have risen sufficiently so that they are light enough to float.

(10) Fry doughnuts on one side in a covered frying pan, turn them and fry on the other side with the lid off.

## Method

Cream yeast with one teaspoon sugar, add a little of the cream (tepid), sprinkle in a pinch of the flour and set in a warm place to 'prove'. When it has risen and bubbles, it is ready for use. Meanwhile whisk together egg yolks and sugar, gradually add the cream, lemon juice, orange juice, lemon rind, rum and salt. Fold in flour, add yeast and finally the melted butter. Beat well with a wooden spoon until dough leaves sides of bowl clean. Sprinkle with a little flour, cover with a cloth and leave in a warm place until about doubled in bulk (about 1 hour). Turn out on to a floured pastry board, cool a little, knead once so that dough is perfectly smooth. Carefully roll out with a rolling pin or press out with your knuckles to about 3mm (⅛in) thickness. Mark half the dough into rounds, cut other half into rounds (about 6cm (2½in) across). Place a little firm apricot jam in centre of marked rounds, cover with cut-out rounds, placing them on the jam upside down (i.e., side that was uppermost should cover jam). Press down edges, and with a smaller circular cutter stamp into rounds. Set on a tray (or baking sheet) covered with a clean cloth sprinkled with flour. Cover lightly with a warmed floured cloth and leave to rise in a warm place.

Use up left-over dough in the same way, adding a little milk if it has become too dry. Test doughnuts very lightly with your fingers and when they feel 'downy' they are ready for frying. Test temperature of fat by sprinkling in a drop of water – if it sizzles properly, fat is the right temperature (the damped handle of a wooden cooking spoon dipped into the fat is another good test). Put doughnuts upside down in the hot fat. Cover frying pan with a lid and fry until one side of doughnuts is deep golden brown.

Lift off lid, turn doughnuts over on other side (sometimes they conveniently turn themselves when one side is fried) and finish frying on other side with the lid off. Drain on paper and dust liberally with icing sugar.

# Guglhupf Aus Germteig I

(For other *Guglhupf* recipes see pages 134, 148 and 155)

Ideally this should be baked in a real *Guglhupf* form (a type of fluted savarin tin) which can on occasion be found in shops specialising in Continental kitchen ware. You can of course use an ordinary savarin tin instead, but a *Guglhupf* form is worth hunting for. I would even venture to say it's worth bringing one back from the Continent, a *Guglhupf* really does taste better when baked in its proper 'setting'. This is not an optical illusion but a matter of simple arithmetic: fluting means an increased surface over which to sprinkle the blanched almonds, a very essential part of this delectable cake! On the Continent, *Guglhupf* forms are generally available in copper, in aluminium, in enamel and more recently also in fireproof glass, but ask any Viennese housewife and she will plump straight for the one made in fireproof pottery, and after all, she should know!

| | |
|---|---|
| 20g (²/₃oz) yeast | Grated lemon rind |
| 3 egg yolks | 50g (2oz) washed and |
| 150g (5¹/₂oz) butter | dried raisins |
| 100g (3oz) sugar | 50g (2oz) blanched almonds |
| ¹/₄ litre (¹/₂ pint) milk | 450g (1lb) flour |

A number of cooks (and very good ones at that) insist that a mixture of half butter and half pure lard gives a better consistency and flavour to their *Guglhupf*. One cook of my acquaintance swears to this day that the only way to get a really satisfactory result is to use one-third of butter, one-third of good margarine and one-third of pure lard. It is greatly a matter of personal taste. You can use half butter and half margarine. Or half butter and half lard (if you are sure of the quality of the lard). Or all margarine. Or half margarine and half lard. But never all lard. And whatever happens, beg, borrow or steal enough butter for the cake tin – it does make all the difference!

# *Austrian* cooking

Cream yeast with 15g (1/2oz) sugar, warm the milk until it is tepid and add a little to the creamed yeast. Stand in a warm place to 'prove'. Butter cake tin well, sprinkle with blanched almonds (cut into thin strips) and dust lightly with flour. (Ground almonds instead of the flour sprinkled over the cake tin greatly enhance the flavour.) Cream the butter and the sugar, gradually add the egg yolks. Add a little of the flour, then the 'proved' yeast and the remainder of the flour alternately with the milk. Beat well either with the hand or with a wooden spoon until dough leaves spoon and sides of bowl clean. Add raisins and a little grated lemon rind. Arrange dough in cake tin, cover with a cloth and leave to rise in a warm place. The cake tin should be about three-quarters filled and the cake left to rise until dough comes to within 1cm (1/2in) of rim of cake tin. Put cake in a hot oven (220°C/425°F/Gas 7), lower heat after about 6 minutes to 200°C/400°F/Gas 6 and a little later to 185–190°C/360–375°F/Gas 41/2–5. Cover top of cake with buttered greaseproof paper if it gets browned too quickly during baking. When baked turn carefully out of tin, leave to cool a little, then sprinkle thickly with vanilla sugar (icing sugar in which a vanilla pod has been kept).

# *Guglhupf Aus Germteig II*

This is sometimes described as 'French *Guglhupf*' in Vienna and is a slightly quicker method.

| | |
|---|---|
| 250g (9oz) flour | 1/2 cup milk |
| 110g (4oz) butter | 3 eggs |
| 1/2 cup blanched almonds | 2 tablespoons sugar |
| 1/2 cup roasted and dried raisins | 15g (1/2oz) yeast |
| | Grated lemon rind |

Sift flour into a warmed bowl. Mix yeast with a little of the sugar and the tepid milk. Make a well in centre of flour and pour in the yeast mixture. Sprinkle with a little flour, cover with a cloth and set in a warm place to 'prove'. Butter a *Guglhupf* mould (or savarin tin). Sprinkle with blanched almonds cut into strips, then sprinkle with flour. Set butter to melt in a warm place. When the yeast mixture begins to bubble, mix yeast into remainder of flour, add remaining sugar and lightly beaten eggs. Beat well with a wooden spoon (or with the hand), gradually adding the melted butter which must not be hot. Beat until mixture leaves spoon and sides of bowl clean. Stir in the raisins and the grated lemon rind. Arrange mixture in prepared cake tin which should be about two-thirds full. Set in a warm place to rise. When mixture has risen to within 1cm (1/2in) of top of cake tin put the cake in a hot oven (220°C/425°F/Gas 7), turn down heat to 190°C/375°F/Gas 5 after 5 minutes (and later to 185°C/360°F/Gas 41/2), without opening oven door. Bake for about 40 minutes in all – you may have to cover top of cake with buttered greaseproof paper in case this browns too quickly. Dust with icing sugar while cake is still warm.

# *Raisin or Sultana Bread*

*Milchbrot*

300g (11oz) flour
50g (2oz) sugar
10g (1/2oz) yeast
40g (11/2oz) butter (melted)
140ml (1/4 pint) milk
1 egg or 2 egg yolks

Pinch salt
Grated lemon rind
1/2 cup washed and dried
  raisins or sultanas
Egg for brushing over pastry
2 tablespoons sugar

Cream yeast with one teaspoon sugar, add half a cup tepid milk. Sprinkle with a little flour and set in a warm place to prove. Sift remaining flour and sugar into a warmed bowl, add egg, melted butter, salt, grated lemon rind and dissolved yeast. Gradually add the remaining milk. Beat well with a wooden spoon until dough is smooth and shiny and leaves sides of the bowl clean. Sprinkle with a little flour and put in a warm place to rise (about 30 minutes). Tip contents of bowl on to a floured pastry board, add the sultanas and divide dough into three equal parts. Shape into long rolls, plait into a loaf. Put the loaf on a buttered and floured baking dish or cake tin, cover with a cloth and leave to rise in a warm place (about 30 minutes). Brush with egg and bake, first at 220°C/425°F/Gas 7 for about 6 minutes, lowering the heat gradually and finish baking at 185°C/360°F/Gas 41/2.

Egg yolk only may be used for this recipe in which case the quantity of milk has to be slightly increased. Top of sultana loaf may be sprinkled with sugar before or after baking. To be eaten sliced, with butter and jam or honey.

# Plaited Coffee Loaf

*Kaffeestriezel*

420g (14oz) flour
15g (1/2oz) yeast
1 teaspoon flour
1/2 teaspoon sugar
50g (2oz) melted butter
225ml (3/8 pint) milk
70g (2 1/2oz) sugar

1 egg and 1 egg yolk
(or 1 large egg)
70g (2–3oz) raisins
1/2 cup blanched almonds
Egg and sugar for brushing
over cake

Cream yeast with half a teaspoon of sugar, add one teaspoon flour and 70ml (1/8 pint) tepid milk and set in a warm place to prove. Sift half the flour into a warmed bowl. Make a well in centre and add the yeast and half the milk. Work dough with a wooden spoon or with your hand until it is perfectly smooth. Sprinkle with a little flour, set in a warm place to rise (about 20 minutes).

Whisk egg (or egg and egg yolk) with sugar, gradually add remaining milk and finally the remaining flour and melted butter. Mix together the two kinds of dough and work well until dough begins to blister. Add the washed and dried raisins, sprinkle with a little flour and leave to rise again (about 1 hour). Sprinkle pastry board with flour, divide dough into three equal parts (it will be very soft and has to be handled rather carefully). Shape each part into a roll and then plait rolls into a loaf. Carefully set loaf in a buttered and floured baking tin and put in a warm place to rise. Brush loaf with egg in which a little sugar has been dissolved and sprinkle with blanched almonds cut into strips. Bake at 185°C/365°F/Gas 4 1/2 for about 35 to 40 minutes.

# *Nut Crescents*

*Nussbeugel*

250g (8oz) flour
125g (4oz) butter
Pinch salt

45g (1½oz) sugar
15g (½oz) yeast
About ½ cup milk

## *Filling*

100g (3½oz) ground walnuts
70g (2½oz) biscuit or cake
  crumbs or grated honeycake
140ml (¼ pint) water
60g (2oz) sugar

A little rum
Grated lemon rind
Cinnamon
Egg for brushing over pastry

Cream yeast with a pinch of sugar, add tepid milk and set to prove in a warm place. Sift together remaining sugar, pinch of salt and flour. Make a little well in the centre and pour in the yeast. Cut the butter into the flour and mix everything to a smooth dough. Divide pastry into 2 or 3 equal lumps and knead each one separately until very smooth. Cover with a cloth and leave for 10 to 15 minutes (do not set to rise). Shape each piece into a roll and cut off small chunks, about 1cm (½in) thick. Flatten these with a rolling pin and spread with filling. Fold over pastry, press together edges and shape into small crescents. Set on a buttered and floured baking sheet and spread with egg yolk. Wait for egg yolk to dry, then brush with egg white. Place in hot oven (225°C/435°F/Gas 7½), lower heat to about 200°C/400°F/Gas 6 about 4 minutes later and bake until golden brown. Crescents will have a 'marbled' finish.

For the filling dissolve sugar in water and bring to boil. Mix together walnuts and crumbs, add lemon rind, cinnamon and a dash of rum. Pour boiling sugar solution over crumbs, etc., and stir well. Leave to cool before using.

# *Poppyseed Crescents*

*Mohnbeugel*

Pastry as for Nut Crescents
  (see previous page)
70ml (1/8 pint) water
140ml (1/4 pint) ground poppy seeds
50g (2oz) sugar

Rum
Grated lemon rind
Cinnamon
Egg for brushing over
  pastry

Dissolve sugar in water, bring to boil and mix with ground poppy seeds. Add rum, grated lemon rind and cinnamon and leave to cool. Fill and bake crescents as described above for Nut Crescents. Cake or biscuit crumbs (or grated honeycake) may partly replace the poppy seeds and honey may be used instead of sugar for sweetening.

# *Nusspotitze*

140g (5oz) butter
70g (2¹/2oz) sugar
3 egg yolks
25g (1oz) yeast

125ml (¹/4 pint) milk
280g (10oz) flour
A little grated lemon rind

## Filling

500g (1lb) walnuts
170g (6oz) sugar
125ml (¹/4 pint) rum
200ml (8fl oz) honey

2 tablespoons raisins
A little grated lemon rind
Lemon juice, cinnamon
70ml (¹/8 pint) cream

Butter and flour a savarin tin. Cream yeast with a little of the sugar, add tepid milk. Add a pinch of flour and set to prove in a warm place. Cream butter and sugar, add yolks. Add flour alternately with yeast and milk. Beat well with a wooden spoon until dough comes away clean from the spoon. Sprinkle pastry board with flour, spread dough over pastry board, cover with the filling, roll up and set in savarin tin. Put in a warm place cover with a cloth and leave to rise for about 40 minutes. Bake at 190°C/375°F/Gas 5 for about 1 hour.

For the filling put all ingredients (except honey and rum) in a bowl. Heat the honey and stir into other ingredients, add the rum.

*Austrian* cooking

# Nut Strudel made with Yeast

*Nuss Strudel*

200g (7oz) flour
1/2 cup milk
Pinch salt
30g (1oz) sugar
1 egg
Grated lemon rind

60g (2oz) melted butter
15g (1/2oz) yeast
15g (1/2oz) flour
1 teaspoon sugar
Egg for brushing over pastry

## Filling

1 tablespoon butter
120g (4oz) ground walnuts
60g (2oz) cake or biscuit crumbs
30g (1oz) sugar
125ml (scant 1/4 pint) milk

A little rum
Grated lemon rind
Cinnamon

Cream yeast with one teaspoon sugar, add a little of the milk (tepid) and 15g (1/2oz) of flour. Set to prove in a warm place. Sift salt, flour and sugar into a warmed mixing bowl, add lemon rind, egg, remainder of milk and dissolved yeast. Finally add the melted butter. Beat well with a wooden spoon until dough leaves sides of bowl clean. Sprinkle with a little flour, cover with a cloth and set to rise in a warm place (1 hour). Tip dough on to floured pastry board, knead very lightly so that dough is perfectly smooth, sprinkle with a little flour and roll out to about 3mm (1/8in) thickness. Spread with filling, roll up as for Swiss roll. Bend into a horseshoe and set on a buttered and floured baking sheet. Cover with a cloth and leave to rise in a warm place for 30 minutes. Brush with egg and bake at 190°C/375°F/Gas 5.

Filling: dissolve sugar and butter in milk, bring to boil and pour over walnuts and crumbs. Mix well, add rum, cinnamon, lemon rind and leave to cool before using.

# Poppyseed Strudel made with Yeast

*Mohnstrudel*

Pastry as for Nut Strudel (see previous page)
Egg for brushing over pastry

## Filling

120g (4oz) ground poppy seeds          30g (1oz) butter
125ml (scant 1/4 pint) milk             60g (2oz) sugar
Grated lemon rind                       Cinnamon
1 tablespoon washed and dried raisins

Prepare in exactly the same way as Nut Strudel. For the filling cook ground poppy seeds in milk until thick. Add butter and sugar and remove from heat. Stir well, adding grated lemon rind and a sprinkling of cinnamon at the same time. Finally stir in the raisins. Cool before using.

# Plum Cake
# made with Yeast

*Zwetschkenkuchen*

150g (5oz) flour
8g (1/4oz) yeast
30g (1oz) sugar
60g (2oz) melted butter
1 egg yolk

Pinch salt
Grated lemon rind
225ml (8fl oz) milk
Plums

## To sprinkle over cake

30g (1oz) sugar
75g (2½oz) flour
30g (1oz) butter

30g (1oz) blanched ground almonds
A little milk or egg white

Cream yeast with a little (about half a cup) of the milk and a pinch of sugar and flour. Set in a warm place to prove. Sift remaining flour with sugar and salt into a warmed mixing bowl, make a well in centre and drop in the egg yolk. Add the milk, grated lemon rind, dissolved yeast, melted butter, and beat well with a wooden spoon until dough is smooth and shiny. Spread on a buttered and floured baking sheet, cover thickly with halved plums (skin side downwards and set to rise in a warm place under a cloth. Meanwhile sift 75g (2½oz) of flour and 30g (1oz) of sugar into a bowl, add the ground almonds and crumble butter into this. Add a few drops milk (or egg white) and when plum cake has well risen (after about 45 minutes), sprinkle this mixture thickly over plums. Bake at 195°C/385°F/Gas 5½, lowering heat towards end of baking time. Sprinkle thickly with sugar when cooled a little.

# *Puff Pastry made with Yeast I*

*Germbutterteig I*

125g (4oz) butter
250g (8oz) flour
25g (1 scant oz) yeast
15g (1/2oz) sugar
1 egg yolk

About 1/2 cup milk
1 teaspoon flour for mixing
  yeast
Pinch salt

Sift flour and salt and divide into two equal parts of 125g (4oz) each. Cut butter into 125g (4oz) of flour, knead a little, shape into a brick and chill.

Cream yeast with sugar, add lukewarm milk and one teaspoon flour and put in a warm place to 'prove'. Sift remaining flour into a warmed bowl, make a little well in centre and drop in the egg yolk. When the yeast begins to throw light bubbles, stir egg yolk into flour, add yeast mixture and knead to a smooth dough. (A little more lukewarm milk may have to be added, this depends entirely on the size of the egg yolk and quality of flour.) Pat yeast dough into a round, cover with a cloth and set to rise for about 15 minutes in a warm place. After that time place dough on a floured pastry board and leave to cool for a little while. Roll out yeast dough to about three times the size of the butter brick. Place butter brick in centre, fold yeast dough over it. Beat with a rolling pin, then roll out to original size. Fold dough into three again, beat with rolling pin, then roll out. Repeat this once more, place pastry in a cool place for 30 minutes before using.

*Austrian* cooking

# Puff Pastry made with Yeast II

*Germbutterteig II*

150g (5oz) flour
Pinch salt
10g (1/3oz) yeast
30g (1oz) melted butter
15g (1/2oz) sugar
1 large egg yolk

1/2 cup milk
1 teaspoon flour for mixing
  yeast
90g (3oz) butter
30g (1oz) flour

Cut 90g (3oz) of butter into 30g (1oz) of flour, shape into a brick and chill.
    Cream yeast with sugar, add lukewarm milk and one teaspoon flour and
set in a warm place to 'prove'. Sift flour with salt, make a well in centre and
drop in the egg yolk. When the yeast begins to 'bubble', add it to the flour,
mix well and stir in the melted butter. Knead well until dough is very smooth.
Sprinkle with a little flour, cover with a cloth and leave for 15 minutes. After
that time, knead dough for 30 seconds so that it is really smooth, then roll
out on a floured pastry board to about three times the size of the butter brick
(dough should be slightly thicker towards the centre). Place chilled butter
brick in centre, fold sides of yeast pastry over butter brick and beat well with
a rolling pin. Roll out pastry to a strip, fold both sides to middle, then fold
pastry in half – rather like closing a book. Cover pastry with a cloth and
leave in a cool place for 30 minutes. Repeat rolling and folding process –
first folding pastry into three parts, rolling it out, then folding it into four parts
and finally folding it over again. Leave dough for 15 minutes (longer if
possible) in a cool place, then use as required.

# Croissants

*Butterkipferl*

Puff pastry made with yeast II
  (page 182)

Egg yolk for brushing over
  pastry

Roll out pastry to a square about 3mm (1/8in) thick. Cut into squares first, then divide squares into triangles. Roll into crescents and set on a buttered and floured baking sheet to rise. When well risen brush over with egg yolk and bake in hot oven until golden brown (195°C/385°F/Gas 5½).

    There are, of course, various ways of embellishing these croissants. You may like to spread a little icing over them while they are still warm or sprinkle them with chopped walnuts or almonds before baking. You can fill them with jam or raisins, grated nuts and chocolate, or you might like to try the following:

# Croissants with Marzipan Filling

*Butterkipferl au Chevalier*

Puff pastry made with yeast II
  (page 182)
2 egg whites
90g (3oz) icing sugar

60g (2oz) ground hazelnuts
A little grated lemon rind
Cinnamon
Egg for brushing over pastry

Roll out pastry to a square about 3mm (1/8in) thick. Cut into squares. Whisk egg whites until stiff, whisk in the sugar, then fold in ground hazel nuts and lemon rind and cinnamon. Place a little of the filling in centre of each square, roll up pastry and shape into crescents. Secure each little 'flap' with a touch of egg. Set crescents on a buttered and floured baking sheet to rise. When doubled in size, brush with egg and bake in hot oven (190°C/ 375°F/Gas 5). Sprinkle with icing sugar when still warm.

*Austrian* cooking

# Marzipan Crescents

*Marzipan Kipferl*

| | |
|---|---|
| Puff pastry made with yeast II (page 182) | 60g (2oz) sugar |
| | 1 egg |
| 125g (1/4lb) blanched almonds (ground) | Egg yolk for brushing over pastry |

Mix together almonds and sugar, work to a smooth paste with the egg. Prepare pastry as described on page 182. Roll out to 3mm (1/8in) thickness and cut into squares. Spread with the almond paste to within 3mm (1/8in) of the edge, roll up and shape into a crescent. Set on a buttered and floured baking sheet, cover with a cloth and set in a warm place to rise. When risen to about double the original size, brush with egg yolk and bake at 190°C/375°F/Gas 5 until golden brown.

# Hazel Nut Rolls

*Haselnuss Rollen*

**(About 25 small rolls)**

| | |
|---|---|
| Puff pastry made with yeast I (page 181) | 1 egg white |
| | Cinnamon |
| 150g (5oz) ground hazel nuts | Grated lemon rind |
| 1 tablepoon honey | Egg yolk for brushing over pastry |
| 1 tablespoon sugar | |
| 15g (1/2oz) grated chocolate | |

Set aside about 15g (1/2oz) ground hazel nuts for sprinkling over pastry. Mix together all other ingredients and work well with a wooden spoon. A little more honey or a few drops milk may have to be added if egg white is too small. Roll out the pastry to about 3mm (1/8in) thickness, cut into squares. Place a little of the hazel nut mixture down the centre of each square, shape into small rolls (brush one side of pastry with egg yolk before folding over second half). Place rolls on a buttered and floured baking sheet and set in

# Cakes, Pastries and Biscuits

a warm place to rise. When risen to about twice their original size, brush with egg yolk, sprinkle with ground hazel nuts and bake in hot oven until golden brown (200°C/400°F/Gas 6).

# Ring Cake

*Kranzkuchen*

Puff pastry made with
  yeast II (page 182)
1 tablespoon melted butter
30g (1oz) ground or chopped
  almonds (not blanched)
1/2 cup washed and dried
  raisins

30g (1oz) grated chocolate
About 1 tablespoon cake
  or biscuit crumbs
Rum
Icing sugar
Cinnamon
Egg for brushing over pastry

Roll out pastry into a rectangular piece, about 3mm (1/8in) thick. Mix together ground or chopped almonds, raisins, grated chocolate, crumbs and about one tablespoon sugar. Sprinkle over rolled-out pastry, then sprinkle with rum, a little cinnamon and finally with the melted butter. Roll up as for Swiss roll. Placing the folded-over edge underneath, twist into a round and set in a buttered and floured cake tin. Secure ends well so that the filling stays sealed in during the baking. Make a few incisions along the top. Cover with a cloth and set in a warm place to rise. When risen to about twice its original size brush with egg and place in hot oven (195°C/385°F/Gas 5 1/2). Bake until deep golden brown, lowering heat towards the end of the baking time (185°C/360°F/Gas 4 1/2). Remove from oven, mix a little icing sugar with a few drops rum and spread over top of cake while still warm but not hot.

# Nut Ring

*Nusskranz*

Puff pastry made with
  yeast II (page 182)
90–120g (3–4oz) ground walnuts
60g (2oz) biscuit crumbs or
  grated honeycake

Grated lemon rind
Cinnamon
A little cream
1 tablespoon sugar
Egg for brushing over pastry

Mix together ground walnuts, biscuit crumbs, grated lemon rind, a little cinnamon, sugar (or honey) and sufficient cream to make a very thick paste (left-over egg white may be used instead of the cream). Roll out pastry to about 3mm (1/8in) thickness, rectangular shape. Cut into three strips. Divide nut filling into three portions and place filling down centre of each strip. Fold over sides of pastry (brush one side with a little egg first before folding over other half). You now have three long rolls of pastry each filled with the nut mixture. Plait rolls very loosely, twist into a ring (side where pastry edges were folded over uppermost) and set in a large buttered and floured cake tin. Cover with a cloth and leave to rise in warm place. Then brush over with egg and bake in hot oven (195°C/385°F/Gas 5 1/2), lowering heat to 180°C/350°F/Gas 4 after about 15 minutes. Brush with icing sugar dissolved in a little rum while still warm and sprinkle with toasted chopped walnuts or almonds.

# 'Snails'

*Schnecken*

Puff pastry made with yeast I
  (page 181)
30g (1oz) raisins (washed and
  dried)
45g (1½oz) ground walnuts

45g (1½oz) sugar
35g (1oz) grated chocolate
30g (1oz) melted butter
Egg for brushing over pastry

Roll out pastry into a rectangular piece, about 6mm (¼in) thick. Mix together dry ingredients and sprinkle over pastry, then sprinkle with melted butter. Roll up as for Swiss roll. Cut into slices about 1cm (½in) thick. Place, cut side down, on a buttered and floured baking sheet. (Take the little flap of pastry where it was folded over and put it underneath each piece.) Leave to rise in a warm place, then brush with egg and bake in a hot oven 195–200°C/390–400°F/Gas 5½–6) until golden brown. Stir a few drops rum into some icing sugar and spread over pastry while still warm but not hot.

# Cream Cheese Pastries

*Topfengolatschen*

Puff pastry made with yeast I
  (page 181)
250g (1/2lb) cream cheese
90g (3oz) sugar
30g (1oz) raisins

2 egg yolks or 1 egg
A little cream
Grated lemon rind
Egg for brushing over
  pastry

Wash and dry raisins. Beat cream cheese with sugar and egg yolks (or egg), stir in sufficient cream to give a thick creamy consistency. Add raisins and grated lemon rind. Roll out pastry to about 3mm (1/8in) thickness. Cut into squares and place a spoonful of the cream cheese filling in centre of each square. Fold all four corners of each square to middle so that filling is completely encased. Secure with a very small round of pastry on top (use pastry cuttings for this). Place pastries on buttered and floured baking sheet and set to rise in a warm place. When well risen brush with egg and bake in hot oven until golden brown (195°C/385°F/Gas 5½). Sprinkle with sugar before serving.

## Cakes, Pastries and Biscuits

# *Fruit Loaves*

*Fruechtenbrot*

150g (5¹/₂oz) flour
15g (¹/₂oz) yeast
Pinch salt
1 egg yolk
A little milk

30g (1oz) sugar
60g (2oz) butter
Egg for brushing over pastry
A few blanched almonds

## Filling

60g (2oz) walnuts
30g (1oz) mixed candied peel
75g (2¹/₂oz) hazel nuts
75g (2¹/₂oz) dates (after stoning)
75g (2¹/₂oz) figs
75g (2¹/₂oz) currants
75g (2¹/₂oz) raisins
140g (5oz) sugar

75g (2¹/₂oz) biscuit crumbs
75ml (¹/₈ pint) rum
30ml (1fl oz) vanilla liqueur (or
  1 or 2 tablespoons Kirsch)
A little grated orange rind
A little lemon juice
30g (1oz) pistachios
75g (2¹/₂oz) almonds (not blanched)

Chop walnuts, pistachios, hazel nuts, dates, figs, almonds and mixed peel.
Put in a bowl, add lemon juice, orange rind, raisins, currants, rum and
vanilla liqueur (or Kirsch). Cover and leave overnight. On the next day add
the sugar and the biscuit crumbs and mix everything together.

Sift flour and salt into a bowl. Dissolve sugar and yeast in about half a
cup of tepid milk and add to flour (do not let it 'prove'). Add the egg yolk
and the butter cut into small pieces. Knead to a dough. Roll out dough on
a floured pastry board as thin as possible. Cut into squares or rectangles.
Place a good portion of the filling in centre of each square, fold over pastry
and secure edges. Place the small loaves (pastry fold underneath) on a
buttered and floured baking sheet, well apart. Brush with egg yolk and leave
to dry in a cool place. When egg yolk has dried, brush with egg white and
decorate with halved blanched almonds. Place in a preheated oven
(180°C/350°F/Gas 4) and bake until golden brown.

*Austrian* cooking

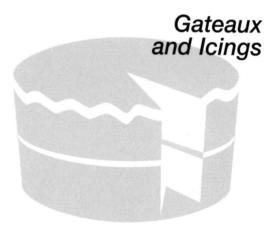

## Gateaux
## and Icings

# Gateaux and Icings

There is no real translation for *Torte*, and for want of a better name I have referred to the recipes in the following chapter as gateaux. That they stand in a group all by themselves no one will dispute. Most significant perhaps is their pristine look, the absence of all superfluous trimmings. No sickly swirls of mock-cream tinted a rich pink, no false pretences – decorations simply are not worn. A smoothly rounded top, a modest sprinkling of grated chocolate or nuts, a preserved cherry or two – that is all. Occasionally, though rarely, a tiny swirl of the good filling that goes inside. As if just that much had been left over and couldn't bear to be wasted...

Some *Torten* are filled and iced, others iced only. Sometimes the filling spreads over top and sides of the gateau as well, or the top may just be dusted with icing sugar. Never be tempted to have several layers when there is only sufficient filling for one good spread – you should be able to taste the filling, not merely guess at its presence!

If at all possible, have a copper bowl for whisking egg whites. Preheat the oven – always. Use a cake tin with a removable bottom so that the cake slides out easily. Cool the cake on a sieve or a rack, upside down. This is important, for the cake should also be iced that way: the absolutely flat part which touched the baking tin uppermost. If the cake has risen too much during the baking, trim it a little so that it stands straight.

# *Austrian* cooking

# *Kathi's Special Roulade*

Kathi is part of the family. She is my mother-in-law's cook in Vienna and has ruled her with a rod of iron for the last 34 years. Her culinary achievements are numerous, but this is my favourite:

*1/4 litre (scant 1/2 pint) milk*
*Pinch of salt and sugar*
*1 rounded dessertspoon*
  *butter*

*2 rounded teaspoons potato*
  *flour*
*2 rounded teaspoons flour*
*4 eggs*

Separate egg yolks and whites. Heat the milk with sugar and salt. Melt the butter, stir in potato flour and flour, do not let it brown. Add the hot milk gradually, stirring all the time, cook until thick. Remove from heat, beat in the egg yolks one by one, and when cooled, fold in stiffly beaten egg whites. Spread on buttered and floured paper and bake until golden brown (190°C/375°F/Gas 5). Turn on a board sprinkled with icing sugar, remove paper and roll pastry lightly over fresh paper sprinkled with sugar.

## *Cream Filling*

*2 tablespoons vanilla sugar*
*3 egg yolks*
*1 teaspoon gelatine*

*A little rum*
*280ml (1/2 pint) cream*

Dissolve gelatine in a little water. Whisk egg yolks with sugar over steam until thickened, remove from heat, add the gelatine and whisk until cool, adding a little rum at the same time. Whisk cream until thick, add a little sugar to taste and fold whipped cream into the egg mixture.

Spread thickly over the pastry and fold over very lightly – do not roll up tightly as for Swiss roll. Spread outside of roll with some more sweetened whipped cream and chill before serving. Kathi hands strawberry purée folded into an equal quantity of whipped cream separately. Did I say that she rules us with a sugared rod of iron?

# Alpenbuttertorte

This is my favourite birthday cake. I do not know where the recipe originally came from, I only know that it has been with my family ever since my great-grandmother could remember!

## Cake

2 eggs
1 egg yolk

70g (2¹/₂oz) icing sugar
60g (2oz) flour

## Cream

¹/₂ cup cream
2 egg yolks
A tiny pinch flour

75g (2¹/₂oz) butter
75g (2¹/₂oz) vanilla sugar

Place eggs, egg yolk and sugar in a bowl and whisk until very thick and creamy. Fold in sifted flour. Bake in a buttered and floured cake tin at 185°C/365°F/Gas 4¹/₂ for about 30 minutes. Cool on rack or on a sieve, then cut once or twice and fill with the following cream:

## Buttercream Filling

Place egg yolks, flour and cream in a bowl and whisk over steam until thick. Remove from heat and whisk until cool. Cream butter and sugar and work in the egg cream in teaspoons.

Cover top and sides of gateau with melted jam, leave to dry, then spread with thin coffee icing. Decorate with glacé cherries.

# *Austrian* cooking

## *Biskottentorte*

Put 100g (3oz) of hazel nuts or almonds (or a mixture of both) on a baking sheet and toast lightly in oven. Grind, then pour over half a cup of hot milk and leave to cool. Cream 100g (3oz) of butter with 100g (3oz) of sugar, gradually work in two egg yolks. Finally add cooled nuts which will by now have become rather mushy. Butter a cake tin. Fill a soup plate with milk, add a few drops rum. Quickly dip some finger biscuits into the milk, taking care that they should not get too wet. Line the cake tin with the sponge fingers, cover with a layer of cream, then with another layer of 'dipped' sponge fingers, a layer of cream, finishing with sponge fingers. Cover with a buttered plate and weigh down. Chill well (overnight if possible, otherwise at least two hours). Slide out cake carefully, cut some sponge fingers to the same height as the gateau and stick around the cake, tie with a ribbon. If possible pile a little whipped cream on top of gateau, sprinkle with grated chocolate or grated toasted almonds or hazel nuts. Alternatively, keep back some of the cream used for filling, spread smoothly over top and sprinkle with toasted almonds, etc., as before.

## *Marbled Cream Slab*

*Bunter Rehruecken*

Whisk two eggs with 60g (2oz) of icing sugar over steam until thick, remove from fire, whisk until cool. Fold in 60g (2oz) of flour. Line a baking sheet with buttered and floured paper, spread with mixture and bake until pale golden brown (190°C/375°F/Gas 5). Remove from baking sheet and take off paper while still warm. Line an oblong buttered cake tin with this pastry, keeping back enough of the pastry to make a 'lid'.

Cream 180g (6oz) of butter with 110g (4oz) of icing sugar. Divide into three parts. Colour one part with a few drops pink culinary colouring, add a little Maraschino. Colour second part green, add a few drops rum. Add 30g (1oz) of melted and cooled chocolate to third part. Spread each layer separately into pastry shell, placing a layer of lightly poached fruit (drained frozen fruit is excellent for this purpose) between each layer of cream. Cover with pastry 'lid'. Chill well. Unmould and spread chocolate icing over top and sides.

# Cream Gateau

*Cremetorte*

100g (3½oz) flour
150g (5½oz) icing sugar

70g (2oz) butter
4 eggs

Separate egg yolks and whites. Keep whites for the filling, also set aside 120g (4½oz) of the icing sugar. Sift together flour and remaining sugar 30g (1oz). Make a well in centre drop in the yolks, crumble butter into flour. Quickly work to a dough and divide into three equal parts. Using a cake tin as a guide, roll pastry into three equal sized rounds, lay on a buttered baking sheet, prick with a fork and bake separately until light golden brown (180°C/350°F/Gas 4). Leave to cool a little, remove carefully from baking sheet. Whisk egg whites until stiff, fold in 60g (2oz) of icing sugar, whisk until smooth. Fold in remaining sugar. Sandwich together cake rounds with this mixture, set carefully on buttered and floured baking sheet and bake at 100°C/200°F/Gas ½ until filling has set. Serve dusted with icing sugar.

*Austrian* cooking

# Dobos Torte

This is a truly luscious layer cake where the thickness of the cream filling should equal that of the pastry. The whole thing is decorated with a crisp brown sugar top.

There is no difficulty in preparing the pastry and a kind patissier even taught me a little trick for a professional finish which I am only too happy to pass on. The sugar top is a little more difficult – you have to work pretty fast and for the first few times you might find it better to aim at *Dobos Schnitten* (Dobos slices) rather than a gateau, as slices are so much easier to cope with.

## For the Gateau

70g (2½oz) icing sugar
3 eggs

60g (2oz) flour

Sift flour twice. Separate egg yolks and whites. Whisk egg yolks with half the sugar until thick. Whip egg whites until stiff, fold in remaining sugar. Fold egg whites into yolks, alternately with the flour. Spread buttered and floured cake tins of equal size thinly with this mixture and bake in preheated oven until golden brown (190°C/375°F/Gas 5) for about 15 minutes. Remove carefully from tins and cool. When quite cold place pastry rounds between sheets of waxed paper, cover with a board and weigh down (the patissier's trick).

For the filling you have the choice of two recipes:

## Dobos Filling I

60g (2oz) butter
60g (2oz) icing sugar

60g (2oz) chocolate
1 egg yolk

Break chocolate into small pieces and set to melt in warm place. Cream butter, add melted but not hot chocolate and sugar, beat well. Add egg yolk, continue stirring until cream is light and fluffy.

## *Dobos Filling II*

2 eggs
60g (2oz) sugar
60g (2oz) chocolate

60g (2oz) butter
30g (1oz) ground toasted hazel
nuts

Break chocolate into small pieces and put in a bowl over steam to soften. When soft, take from heat, stir once or twice, add sugar and eggs. Return to steam and whip until thick and creamy. Remove from steam, whisk until cool. Cream butter, add chocolate cream gradually, finally stir in the toasted hazel nuts.

Trim pastry rounds and spread with the cream. Set aside one round for the top on a board very lightly dusted with flour. Dissolve 65g (2½oz) sugar in one tablespoon water over a low heat, add a small knob of butter and cook until sugar colours pale golden brown. Remove from heat, cool a little, then spread quickly over top sheet of pastry. Mark into slices at once with a knife frequently dipped into hot water. Replace top on gateau, spread a little chocolate cream round sides.

If sugar top has hardened too quickly, place pastry round oven for a few seconds to soften, then mark as described before.

# Strawberry Gateau

*Erdbeer Kuchen*

60g (2oz) blanched ground almonds
90g (3oz) butter
90g (3oz) sugar
3 eggs
45g (1½oz) flour
45g (1½oz) biscuit or cake crumbs
500g (1lb) strawberries (wild
  strawberries for preference)

120g (4oz) icing sugar
A few drops Maraschino and
  lemon juice
Redcurrant jelly
Glacé fruit
Thin water icing (see
  page 218)

Separate egg yolks and whites. Cream butter and sugar, add the egg yolks. Fold in stiffly beaten egg whites, alternately with the ground almonds, flour and crumbs. Bake in a well-buttered and floured cake tin at 185°C/365°F/Gas 4½. Remove from tin while still warm, cut once when cold.

Dust the strawberries with icing sugar and pass through a sieve. Add a few drops maraschino and lemon juice, bind with redcurrant jelly. Fill cake with two-thirds of this purée, pile remaining purée on top of cake. Sprinkle with glacé fruit (chopped) and cover the whole cake with thin white water icing. Alternately you can arrange a layer of halved strawberries on top of the purée and mix your icing with lemon juice instead of water which gives a pleasant sharp tang.

# Semolina Cake

*Griess Torte*

105g (3½oz) icing sugar
3 eggs
35g (1 generous oz) blanched
  ground almonds

A little lemon juice and
  grated lemon rind
50g (2oz) semolina

Separate egg yolks and whites. Add lemon juice to yolks and whisk with icing sugar until thick, fold in stiffly beaten egg whites alternately with semolina and ground almonds. Add lemon rind. Bake in a well-buttered and floured cake tin at 185°C/365°F/Gas 4½. Cover cake with melted jam and thin lemon icing.

# Hazel Nut Gateau I

*Haselnusstorte I*

4 eggs
55g (2oz) ground hazel nuts
55g (2oz) icing sugar

25g (1oz) melted butter
35g (1½oz) flour
Whipped cream

Separate egg yolks and whites. Whisk egg yolks with sugar until thick. Fold in stiffly beaten egg whites alternately with the hazel nuts and the flour, finally add melted butter. Divide mixture and bake in two separate sandwich tins (190°C/375°F/Gas 5) until golden brown. Remove from tins while still hot, leave to cool on a rack. Sandwich the two halves together with a generous quantity of sweetened whipped cream into which you have folded 1 or 2 tablespoons of toasted, ground hazel nuts.

Top with whipped cream, sprinkle with toasted ground hazel nuts.

# *Austrian* cooking

## Hazel Nut Gateau II

*Haselnusstorte II*

70g (2¹/2oz) sugar
4 eggs

70g (2¹/2oz) toasted hazel nuts
35g (1¹/2oz) breadcrumbs

### Filling

75ml (scant ¹/8 pint) milk
50g (2oz) sugar
25g (1oz) hazel nuts

2 egg yolks or 1 egg
¹/2 teaspoon flour,
40g (1¹/2oz) butter

For the cake, separate egg yolks and whites of three eggs. Whisk egg yolks, whole egg and sugar until thick, fold in stiffly beaten whites alternately with the ground toasted hazel nuts and breadcrumbs. Bake at 180°C/350°F/Gas 4 for about 40 minutes.

When cold cut once or twice and fill either with jam or the following cream: Cook all ingredients except the butter on top of a double-boiler, stirring all the time. Mixture must not boil. Remove when thickened, stir until cool, add to creamed butter. Dust top of gateau with icing sugar.

## Coffee Cream Gateau I

*Kaffeecremetorte I*

75g (2¹/2oz) hazel nuts
75g (2¹/2oz) blanched almonds

150g (5oz) icing sugar
3 egg whites

### Cream

4 tablespoons strong black coffee
120g (4oz) icing sugar

3 egg yolks
100g (3¹/2oz) butter

Place hazel nuts on a baking sheet and put in hot oven (200°C/400°F/Gas 6) for a few minutes. Rub in a tea towel until all the skins come away. Toast almonds lightly in oven. Grind almonds and hazel nuts and mix together. Whisk egg whites until stiff, whisk in half the sugar, fold in remaining sugar lightly. Fold in almonds and hazel nuts. Bake in two separate cake tins until pale golden brown, 190°C/375°F/Gas 5, about 20 to 25 minutes. (This mixture is rather delicate while hot and stiffens quickly as it cools – in order to avoid crumbling or breakage use a cake tin with a removable bottom.) Remove cakes from tins while still hot, leave to cool on a rack. Sandwich together with the following cream, spreading it also over top and sides:

Whisk egg yolks with coffee and sugar over steam until thick. Remove from heat and cool, stirring from time to time. Cream butter and add the egg-cream by the spoonful. Alternately, if real cream is available, use as filling sweetened whipped cream to which a dash of very strong black coffee has been added.

# *Coffee Cream Gateau II*

*Kaffeecremetorte II*

### *(Made with egg whites only)*

| | |
|---|---|
| 3 egg whites | 90g (3oz) icing sugar |
| 90g (3oz) ground blanched almonds | 15g (1/2oz) breadcrumbs |

### *Cream*

| | |
|---|---|
| 1 egg white | 75g (2 1/2oz) sugar |
| 75ml (1/8 pint) strong black coffee | |

Whisk egg whites, fold in icing sugar and whisk again. Fold in blanched almonds and breadcrumbs. Divide mixture into two equal parts, bake separately (190°C/375°F/Gas 5) for about 30 minutes.

When cold sandwich together with the following cream, spreading it also over top and sides of gateau. Sprinkle with chopped toasted hazel nuts:

Dissolve sugar in coffee over low heat. Increase heat and bring sugar solution to 115°C/240°F. Whisk egg white until stiff. Pour boiling sugar solution over egg white, whisking all the time Beat until cool.

For a slightly different version brush each cake round on both sides with strong black coffee to which a dash of rum has been added, then sandwich together with cream as above.

*Austrian* cooking

# Chestnut Gateau I

*Kastanientorte I*

70g (2¹/2oz) butter
70g (2¹/2oz) sugar
3 egg yolks
2 egg whites

100g (3¹/2oz) cooked, sieved chestnuts,
  weighed after sieving
30g (1¹/2oz) grated chocolate

## Cream

60g (2oz) sugar
2 egg yolks
2 tablespoons cream

50g (1¹/2oz) chocolate
90g (3oz) butter

Cream butter with sugar, add egg yolks gradually. Stir in grated chocolate,
then fold in stiffly whipped egg whites alternately with the chestnuts. Bake in
buttered tin at 180°C/350°F/Gas 4. Leave in cake tin for a little to cool,
slide out carefully. For the cream whisk together egg yolks and top milk over
steam until thick, remove from heat and whisk until cool. Melt chocolate
cream butter and stir in melted chocolate. (Chocolate must not be hot and
should be only just spreadable.) Add egg mixture very gradually. Cut cake
once or twice, fill with cream and dust top with icing sugar.

# Chestnut Gateau II

*Kastanientorte II*

70g (2¹/2oz) icing sugar
3 eggs

70g (2¹/2oz) chestnuts weighed after
  boiling, peeling and sieving
35g (1¹/2oz) fine breadcrumbs

## Filling

140ml (¹/4 pint) cream
50g (2oz) chestnuts weighed after
boiling, peeling and sieving

Sugar to taste

Separate egg yolks and whites. Whisk egg yolks with sugar until thick and pale yellow in colour. Fold in stiffly beaten egg whites alternately with chestnuts and breadcrumbs. Bake at 180°C/350°F/Gas 4 for about 40 minutes.

For the filling whip cream until stiff, fold in chestnuts and a little sugar to taste. Cut cake once and fill with cream, spreading it also over top and sides.

# Linzertorte

There are many, many versions of this very popular recipe which is a jam tart rather than a gateau. You could choose from *Linzertorte weiss* (white *Linzertorte*) made either with blanched almonds or without almonds altogether, or *Linzertorte braun* (brown *Linzertorte*) where almonds or nuts play a prominent part.

Then there is *Linzertorte geruehrt*, which means that butter is creamed before the dry ingredients are added rather than crumbling the butter into the dry ingredients. And so it goes on. There is even supposed to be a 'real and genuine' *Linzertorte* originating in the town of Linz (the supposed birthplace of the cake), but rumour has it that this is far, far inferior to all 'copies'!

140g (5oz) sugar
140g (5oz) flour
140g (5oz. butter
140g (5oz) ground almonds
  (not blanched)
Juice of 1/2 lemon

Pinch powdered cloves
  and cinnamon
2 egg yolks or 1 egg
Jam for filling
Egg for brushing
  over pastry

Mix together all dry ingredients. Cut butter into small pieces, crumble into dry ingredients, add egg yolks (or egg). Quickly work to a dough, chill for a little. Roll out two-thirds of the pastry, line bottom and sides of a buttered and floured flan case with this. Spread with good jam, arrange a criss-cross pattern over the top with the remaining pastry. Brush over with egg and bake at 190°C/375°F/Gas 5. When cold dust thickly with icing sugar.

*Austrian* cooking

## Linzertorte *(Creamed Method)*

*Geruehrte Linzertorte*

175g (6oz) butter
90g (3oz) sugar
1 egg
200g (7oz) flour

60g (2oz) ground almonds,
   walnuts or hazelnuts
A little grated lemon rind
Jam

Cream butter and sugar, add egg and continue creaming. Work in flour, almonds, etc., and lemon rind. Spread half of this mixture in a buttered and floured cake tin. Cover with a round of rice paper cut to fit and spread with jam to within 2cm (3/4in) of the edge. With the help of a forcing bag pipe the remaining mixture round the edge, also pipe a criss-cross pattern over the jam. Bake at 180°C/350°F/Gas 4 for about 45 minutes. Dust with icing sugar when cold.

## Meran Gateau

*Meraner Torte*

140g (5oz) butter
140g (5oz) icing sugar
3 eggs
140g (5oz) ground almonds
  (not blanched)

50g (2oz) grated chocolate
Pinch cinnamon and
  powdered cloves

Separate egg yolks and whites. Cream butter and sugar, add egg yolks gradually. Fold in stiffly beaten egg whites alternately with the remaining ingredients. Bake at 185°C/365°F/Gas 4 1/2 for about 40 minutes. When cold spread top and sides with hot jam and cover with chocolate icing.

# *Muerbe Torte I*

180g (6oz) butter
110g (4oz) hazel nuts
110g (4oz) sugar

210g (7oz) flour
1 teaspoon baking powder

Sift together flour and baking powder, sift again, then add sugar. Cut butter into small pieces, crumble into flour and sugar. Add hazel nuts and quickly work to a dough. Divide into three equal parts and bake separately (190°C/375°F/Gas 5). Fill with cream as for *Nusstorte* (see next page) or *Panamatorte* (see page 207). Dust top with icing sugar.

# *Muerbe Torte II*

150g (5oz) flour
150g (5oz) butter
2 hard-boiled egg yolks

Rind of 1/2 lemon
60g (2oz) icing sugar
Jam for filling

Sift dry ingredients, cut butter into small pieces and crumble into dry ingredients. Divide dough into two equal portions, roll into rounds and bake separately. When cold sandwich together with jam and dust top thickly with icing sugar. Mashed and sugared raspberries are a good alternative filling to jam.

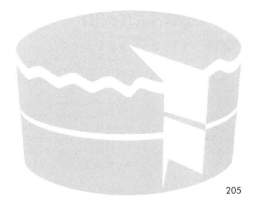

Austrian cooking

# Nut Gateau

*Nusstorte*

3 eggs
70g (2½oz) sugar
70g (2½oz) ground walnuts

A little rum
30g (1oz) fine breadcrumbs

## Cream

60g (2oz) ground walnuts
50g (2oz) sugar
3 egg yolks

125ml (¼ pint) cream
Dash rum

Separate egg yolks and whites. Whisk yolks with sugar, moisten breadcrumbs with rum. Fold stiffly beaten egg whites into yolks, alternately with walnuts and breadcrumbs. Bake in buttered and floured cake tin (185°C/365°F/Gas 4½) for about 40 minutes. When cool, cut once or twice and fill with the following cream:

Put cream, sugar and walnuts in a thick saucepan, cook gently until thick. Remove from heat, turn into a bowl and stir until cool. Whisk in egg yolks and rum. Spread top and sides of cake with hot jam, cover with thin lemon or rum icing, decorate with nuts. Halved walnuts, previously dipped in caramel sugar, make a nice decoration.

# Orange Gateau

*Orangentorte*

3 eggs
Juice and grated rind of ½ orange

125g (4½oz) icing sugar
125g (4½oz) ground, blanched almonds

Separate egg yolks and whites. Whisk egg yolks with 75g (3oz) icing sugar to ribbon stage. Add orange juice and whisk again. Whisk egg whites until stiff, add remaining icing sugar and whisk until smooth. Fold egg whites into yolks alternately with ground almonds. Bake at 180°C/350°F/Gas 4 for about 35 minutes. When cold, cover with hot jam, spread orange icing over top. Decorate with orange sections dipped into sugar boiled to 'soft ball' stage.

# *Panamatorte*

## *Cake*

50g (2oz) chocolate
3 eggs
75g (2¹/2oz) icing sugar

75g (2¹/2oz) ground almonds (not blanched)

## *Cream*

30g (1oz) chocolate
75g (2¹/2oz) butter
75g (2¹/2oz) sugar

1 egg
About 30g (1oz) toasted almonds

Grate chocolate and mix with ground almonds. Separate egg yolks and whites. Whisk egg yolks with 50g (2oz) sugar until thick and creamy. Whip egg whites until stiff, fold in remaining sugar and whisk again until smooth. Fold egg whites into egg yolks, alternately with chocolate-almond mixture. Bake in buttered and floured cake tin at 180°C/350°F/Gas 4 for about 1 hour.

When cold, cut once or twice and fill with the following cream (leaving enough cream to cover top and sides of gateau). Break chocolate into small pieces and put in warm place to melt. Cream butter and sugar, add softened chocolate and beat in the egg. Beat mixture really well, it should be quite thick and fluffy. Sprinkle top and sides of gateau (after spreading with cream) with toasted and coarsely chopped almonds.

# Easter Gateau

*Ostertorte*

3 eggs
65g (2½oz) sugar

65g (2½oz) ground blanched
  almonds
40g (1½oz) flour

## Cream

1 egg
50g (2oz) sugar

45g (1½oz) butter
50g (2oz) chocolate

Separate egg yolks and whites. Whisk egg yolks with sugar until thick and creamy. Whip egg whites until stiff. Fold beaten egg whites into egg yolks, alternately with ground almonds and flour. Bake at 185°C/365°F/Gas 4½ in a buttered and floured cake tin for about 40 minutes. When cold, cut and fill with the following cream:

Whip egg and sugar over steam until thick. Remove from heat and whisk until cool. Cream butter, add softened chocolate and finally add egg mixture very gradually. Spread top and sides of gateau with hot jam, cover with chocolate icing.

# *Whitsun Gateau*

*Pfingsttorte*

## Cake

80g (2¹/₂oz) sugar
80g (2¹/₂oz) blanched almonds,
  ground finely

3 egg yolks
2 egg whites

## Cream

1 egg white
80g (2¹/₂oz) sugar

70ml (¹/₈ pint) water
1 dessertspoon rum

Whisk egg yolks with sugar, fold in stiffly beaten egg whites alternately with the ground almonds. Bake in buttered and floured cake tin for about 35 minutes (185°C/365°F/Gas 4¹/₂). Turn out of tin and cool on a rack.

   Prepare filling by dissolving sugar in water over low heat. Increase heat and cook to 115°C/240°F. Whisk egg white until stiff in a separate bowl while sugar cooks. Pour hot sugar solution on to stiffly beaten egg white, whisking all the time. Add rum and whisk until smooth. Cut cake once or twice, fill with this cream and dust top with sugar.

*Austrian* cooking

# Pischinger Torte

This consists of special round wafers sandwiched together with chocolate cream, the recipe for which is given below. In Austria most of these wafers were manufactured by a firm called Pischinger – hence the name. The wafers are obtainable in some shops under the name of *Karlsbader Oblaten*.

| | |
|---|---|
| 70g (2¹/₂oz) chocolate | 60g (2oz) butter |
| 2 tablespoons water | 1 egg yolk |
| 70g (2¹/₂oz) icing sugar | 60g (2oz) almonds |

Toast almonds lightly in oven, grind. Break chocolate into small pieces, add water and melt over low heat or over steam. Stir, remove from heat and leave to cool. Cream butter and sugar, stir in yolk and melted chocolate and finally 30g (1oz) ground almonds. Spread wafers with this cream and sandwich together. Leave top untouched, but spread cream over sides. Sprinkle sides with remaining ground almonds.

# Punch Gateau

*Punsch Torte*

| | |
|---|---|
| 4 eggs | 2 tablespoons rum |
| 80g (3oz) sugar | Juice 1 orange |
| 80g (3oz) flour | 70ml (¹/₈ pint) water |
| 20g (1 scant oz) butter | A few drops Maraschino |
| 75g (3oz) lump sugar | 1 tablespoon apricot jam |

Whisk eggs and sugar until thick and creamy, fold in sifted flour. Finally stir in melted butter. Bake at 180°C/350°F/Gas 4 for about 40 minutes.

When quite cold cut through twice (the middle layer should be slightly thicker). Spread inside of top and bottom slice with jam. Cut middle layer into small cubes. Rub lump sugar on orange rind, then put sugar, water, rum, maraschino and orange juice in a saucepan and bring to boil. Pour over the cake cubes, add the jam and mix well. Fill cake with this mixture, press down lightly and glaze with hot jam. Cover top and sides with pink icing.

# *Paulinentorte*

My family used to declare with great pride that this recipe was invented by and named after an aunt of mine. As her name really was Paula and, furthermore, as she was very partial to chocolate gateau, this may well be true. I have certainly never come across this recipe anywhere else in fact, the only record I have of it was written in the self-same aunt's own handwriting...

35g (1 generous oz) ground almonds (not blanched)
25g (1 scant oz) breadcrumbs
1 tablespoon rum

50g (2oz) grated chocolate
Rind and juice 1/2 lemon
70g (2oz) icing sugar
3 eggs

Separate egg yolks and whites. Place breadcrumbs in a bowl, moisten with the rum. Sprinkle ground almonds and grated chocolate over the top. Whisk egg yolks with the sugar until thick, add lemon juice and rind. Whip egg whites until stiff, fold into yolks alternately with the other ingredients. Bake for about 40 minutes at 185°C/365°F/Gas 4 1/2. Cover with chocolate icing.

One day, by mistake, I used Maraschino instead of rum for moistening the breadcrumbs. With due apologies to my late aunt (who was a far, far better cook than I can ever hope to be) this was considered a great improvement...

# *Austrian* cooking

## *Sachertorte*

There are a great many myths surrounding the famous *Sachertorte*. One, that it was invented by the now almost legendary Frau Anna Sacher. This is untrue, for it was the founder of the Sacher dynasty, Franz Sacher, who created it in the days when he was still a chef. Herr Sacher is supposed to have said soon afterwards: 'He bothered me and bothered me to invent something new. As if my patisserie were not good enough. So what could I do – I just flung together some ingredients – and there you are.' ('He' was Herr Sacher's employer, Prince Metternich.) Which just goes to show what the 'fling' of a master hand can produce.

Myth number two is that the recipe is a secret held only by the House of Demel. It is quite true that Demel are the sole *concessionnaires* allowed to fix the 'Genuine *Sachertorte*' seal (in finest chocolate) upon their merchandise, but the recipe itself is no longer secret. It was published in full (with permission of Mr Eduard Sacher, Jnr) in *Die Wiener Konditorei* by Hans Skrach (Verlag fuer Jugend und Volk, Vienna), quoting among other ingredients, eighteen egg whites and fourteen egg yolks!

Of course, no self-respecting Viennese will agree that it is the real recipe. Every one of them will assure you that their own version (passed down from grandmother) is the one and only one. I make no such claim... though of course my grandmother once told me... but we shall not go into that! Now if you were to compare my *Sachertorte* with the one bought at Demel...

*150g (5oz) chocolate*
*6 eggs*
*150g (5oz) butter*

*150g (5oz) icing sugar*
*120g (4 generous oz) flour*

Sift flour twice. Separate egg yolks and whites. Break chocolate into small pieces, add a tablespoon of water and put in a warm place to melt. (Some cooks maintain that rum or Madeira should be used instead of the water and that it should only be added after the chocolate has melted.) Cream butter with 120g (4oz) of sugar, add egg yolks gradually. Add the melted chocolate (which must be soft but not hot) and stir well. Whisk egg whites until stiff, whisk in remaining 30g (1oz) sugar. Fold stiffly beaten egg whites into butter/chocolate mixture alternately with the flour. Bake in buttered and floured 24cm (9½in) cake tin at 180°C/350°F/Gas 4 for about 60 minutes. When cold spread with warmed apricot jam.

# Gateaux and Icings

For the chocolate icing break 120g (4oz) of plain chocolate into small pieces, put to melt in oven. Dissolve 120g (4oz) of sugar in 75ml (3fl oz) of water and cook to 'small thread' stage. Remove from heat and leave to cool. Stir lukewarm sugar solution into melted chocolate, add a drop of good olive oil. Stir constantly until mixture has thickened sufficiently to spread over gateau.

Two things should be noted above all others with *Sachertorte*: the gateau should not be very high and the thickness of the icing should about equal that of the apricot jam. It is not true that whipped cream is always served with *Sachertorte*, no one in Vienna will heap it on your *Sachertorte* without asking you first whether you like it. It is, however, true that whipped cream is very, very good with *Sachertorte*.

## My Own Method

I had always been warned that a fate worse than death would befall my *Sachertorte* if I did not follow these instructions implicitly and to the last flick of the egg whisk. Somehow I held a strong distrust for that particular 'old cooks' tale'. Perhaps because I kept remembering Sacher's supposed comment about the 'flinging together' of ingredients. So one day I decided that it was time I had a little culinary fling of my own and this is how I made my *Sachertorte* (ingredients as before):

I broke the chocolate into small pieces, put them in a large fireproof bowl with the water to melt in a warm oven. When the chocolate had softened I added the butter (cut up into smallish pieces) and put the bowl back into the oven for another minute, until the butter was just soft, but not 'oily'. I then retrieved the bowl from the oven, inserted a rotary egg whisk into the mixture and began whisking, adding egg yolks and sugar gradually. I continued whisking until the mixture was light and frothy, then folded in the stiffly beaten egg whites and the flour alternately. The cake was baked as described before. And very good it was too – not to say anything of the time saved in preparation...

*Austrian* cooking

# Cream Cheese Gateau

*Topfentorte*

Prepare shortcrust pastry with 60g (2oz) of sugar, 120g (4oz) of butter and 180g (6oz) of flour, one egg yolk and a little grated lemon rind. Line a buttered and floured cake tin with pastry and bake 'blind'.

Cream 250g (8oz) of cream cheese with 90g (3oz) of sugar, beat in three egg yolks and a little grated lemon rind. Gradually add 200ml (3/8 pint) of milk, finally fold in three stiffly beaten egg whites and 140g (5oz) flour. Pile into the baked pastry shell, sprinkle with 60g (2oz) of washed raisins. Bake for about 1 hour (170°C/325°C/Gas 3).

# *Chocolate Gateau with Almonds I*

*Schokoladetorte mit Mandeln I*

75g (2¹/2oz) chocolate
140g (5oz) icing sugar
75g (2¹/2oz) blanched almonds,
  finely ground

100g (3¹/2oz) butter
4 eggs
45g (1¹/2oz) flour
A little grated lemon rind

Separate egg yolks and whites. Break chocolate into small pieces and put in a warm place to melt. Sift together ground almonds with half the sugar. Cream butter and remaining sugar, add egg yolks gradually. Whisk egg whites until stiff, fold into creamed butter alternately with sugar-almonds and flour. Sprinkle in grated lemon rind. Bake for about 45 minutes at 185°C/365°F/Gas 4¹/2. When cold spread with warmed jam and cover with chocolate icing.

# Gateaux and Icings

# *Chocolate Gateau with Almonds II*

*Schokoladetorte mit Mandeln II*

3 eggs
70g (2¹/₂oz) sugar

70g (2¹/₂oz) grated chocolate
70g (2¹/₂oz) ground almonds

Separate egg yolks and whites. Whisk egg yolks with 60g (2oz) of sugar until thick and creamy. Whisk egg whites until stiff, add remaining sugar and whisk until smooth. Fold egg whites into yolks, alternately with ground almonds and grated chocolate. Bake at 185°C/365°F/Gas 4¹/₂ for about 35 minutes. Cover with hot jam and chocolate icing.

# *Traunkirchner Torte*

Bake three rounds of pastry as for *Muerbe Torte* (see page 205). Sandwich together with the following cream, decorating top of gateau with it as well:
    Sieve a 125g (¹/₄lb) of wild strawberries, stir in 125g (4oz) of icing sugar. Add a teaspoon powdered gelatine previously dissolved in a little hot water and fold in a 140ml (¹/₄ pint) of whipped cream.

# Morello Cherry Gateau

*Weichselcremetorte*

## Cake

65g (2¹/2oz) chocolate
3 eggs
65g (2¹/2oz) melted butter

65g (2¹/2oz) sugar
50g (2oz) flour

## Cream

1 egg yolk
105g (3¹/2oz) sugar
100g (3oz) butter

25g (1oz) chocolate
1 teaspoon brandy or rum
Chopped morello cherries

Grate chocolate and set to melt in warm place. Separate egg yolks and whites. Whisk together egg yolks with half of the sugar. Whip egg whites until stiff. Whisk remaining sugar into egg whites, fold egg whites into yolks. Carefully fold in flour, finally add melted butter and chocolate which should be melted but not hot. Bake in buttered and floured cake tin at 180°C/350°F/Gas 4 for about 40 minutes.

For the cream, whisk egg yolk with 25g (1oz) of sugar over steam until thick. Cream butter with remaining sugar, add egg mixture gradually. Add melted (but not hot) chocolate and rum (or brandy). Divide mixture into two parts. Fold chopped morello cherries into one half. Cut cake in half and spread with this cream, replace top. Spread over top and sides with remaining cream, decorate with stoned morello cherries.

# Soft Chocolate Gateau

*Weiche Schokoladetorte*

40g (1½oz) butter
40g (1½oz) sugar
5 eggs

40g (1½oz) almonds (not
  blanched)
75g (2½oz) chocolate

Separate egg yolks and whites of four eggs. Grate chocolate, grind almonds. Cream butter with 25g (1oz) of sugar, add egg yolks and egg gradually. Whisk egg whites until stiff, whisk in remaining sugar. Fold whipped egg whites into butter mixture, alternately with the ground almonds and grated chocolate. Bake in buttered and floured cake tin for about 1 hour (185°C/365°F/Gas 4½). When cool spread with warmed jam and cover with chocolate icing.

# White Almond Cake

*Weisse Mandeltorte*

3 egg whites
100g (3oz) icing sugar

100g (3oz) blanched almonds,
  finely ground

Whisk egg whites until stiff, whisk in half the sugar. Fold in remaining sugar alternately with the almonds. Bake in a buttered and figured cake tin for about 35 minutes (180°C/350°F/Gas 4). When cold spread with hot jam, cover with lemon water icing.

# *Austrian* cooking

## *Zebra Gateau*

*Zebra Torte*

3 egg yolks
110g (4oz) sugar
110g (4oz) ground blanched almonds

2 egg whites
50g (2oz) chocolate

Whisk egg yolks with sugar, fold in ground almonds and stiffly beaten egg whites. Pour half of this mixture into a buttered floured cake tin. Cover with a round of rice paper which fits exactly. Fold grated chocolate into remaining mixture, spread over mixture in cake tin and bake at 180°C/350°F/Gas 4 for about 40 minutes. When cold, separate two halves carefully, sandwich together with jam and cover with thin lemon water icing.

## *Icings*

(For Chocolate Icing see *Sachertorte*, page 213)

With the exception of *Dobos Torte*, top and sides of all iced gateaux (and most pastries and cakes as well) should be spread with warm jam before the icing is applied. This procedure is called *aprikotieren* in Austria, since the jam is invariably apricot jam, though in fact any smooth jam can be used and I have always found redcurrant jelly excellent for this purpose.

The simplest of all icings is the so-called water icing, where the water is frequently replaced by lemon juice or rum or coffee. Sieve the icing sugar and add a very little water. Do not stir and leave it to stand for about 10 minutes, then stir in the required flavouring (orange juice, lemon juice, liqueur, coffee, rum, etc.), add a little more sugar or liquid to obtain a smooth thick paste, which is then spread over the cake. An even simpler version is to stir the liquid into the sieved sugar, with or without any water added, depending on the strength of the flavour required. It is impossible to give quantities as this is solely a question of the water content in the sugar. This type of icing is best for pastries of all kinds and small cakes, but can be used quite successfully for gateaux.

Fondant icing is a different matter altogether and it is best to make a quantity of fondant to store and use as required. For this the sugar has to be cooked to a 'medium blow' stage which is about 113°C/235°F on the sugar thermometer. To test, dip a small wire loop (I use the rounded end of a skewer) into the hot sugar solution, hold it up, blow on it, and medium-sized bubbles should fly off.

Dissolve 500g (1lb) of lump or granulated sugar in 250ml (½ pint) of water, together with one teaspoon glucose and one teaspoon vinegar. Brush inside of saucepan with a pastry brush previously dipped into cold water, skim off any impurities which rise to the top. As soon as all the sugar has dissolved, increase the heat and bring solution to boil – do not stir. Test as described before and as soon as the 'medium blow' stage is reached, remove saucepan from heat. Pour sugar on to a marble slab, previously sprinkled with water, sprinkling a little cold water over top of sugar as well. Alternatively, simply sprinkle sugar solution in saucepan with cold water. Leave to cool, then work sugar with a spatula or a spoon until white and firm. Knead a little with the hands until fondant becomes pliable. Store in a jar, covered with a damp cloth.

To use fondant: Warm a sufficient quantity of fondant, stirring constantly. This is best done in a bowl over steam, as the fondant must not get hot. Add required flavouring and, if necessary, a little warm water, or sugar solution.

# Austrian cooking

## *By Way of a Summary*

(from *Der Phaake* by Josef Weinheber)
By permission of Hoffmann & Campe Verlag, Hamburg

Ich hab sonst nix, drum hab ich gern
ein gutes Papperl, liebe Herrn:
Zum Gabelfruehstueck goenn ich mir
ein Tellerfleisch, ein Kruegerl Bier,
schieb an und ab ein Gollasch ein,
(kann freilich auch ein Bruckfleisch sein),
ein saftiges Beinfleisch, nicht zu fett,
sonst hat man zu Mittag sein Gfrett.
Dann mach ich – es is eh nicht lang
mehr auf Mittag – mein' Gesundheitsgang,
geh uebern Grabn, den Kohlmarkt aus
ins Michaeler Bierwirtshaus.
Ein Huehnersupperl, tadellos,
ein Beefsteak in Madeirasoss,
ein Schweinspoerkelt, ein Rehragout,
Omletts mit Chamgignon dazu,
hernach ein bisserl Kipfelkoch
und allenfalls ein Torterl noch,
zwei Seidel Goess – zum Trinken mag
ich nicht viel nehmen zu Mittag –
ein Flascherl Gumpolds, nicht zu kalt,
und drei, vier Glaserl Wermuth halt.
Damit ichs recht verdauen kann,
zuend ich mir ein Trabukerl an
und lehn mich z'rueck und schau in d' Hoeh,
bevor ich auf mein' Schwarzen geh.
Wann ich dann heimkomm, will ich Ruh,
weil ich ein Randerl schlafen tu,
damit ich mich, von zwei bis vier,
die Decken ueber, rekreier'.
Zur Jausen geh ich in die Stadt
und schau, wer schoene Stelzen hat,

## *By Way of a Summary*

ein kaltes Ganserl, jung und frisch,
ein Alzerl Kaes, ein Stueckl Fisch,
well ich so frueh am Nachmittag
nicht schon was Warmes essen mag.
Am Abend, muss ich Ihnen sagn,
ess ich gern leicht, wegn meinen Magn,
Hirn in Aspik, Kalbsfrikassee,
ein kleines Zuengerl mit Pueree,
Faschierts und hin und wieder wohl
zum Selchfleisch Kraut, zum Rumpsteak Kohl,
erst spaeter dann, beim Wein zur Not,
ein nett garniertes Butterbrot.
Glaubn S' nicht, ich koennt ein Fresser wern,
ich hab sonst nix, drum leb ich gern...

. . . Since I've nought else, I can enjoy
My victuals all the more my boy:
Elevenses – I don't deny
Myself some meat and beer, and why,
Occasionally, not include
A Goulash? (*Bruckfleisch* too is good),
And juicy beef, though not too greasy
Lest midday find one feeling queasy.
Then for a stroll, a turn or two,
Across the City Ditch, and through
The Kohlmarkt – that's enough if I'm
To reach the Bierwirtshaus in time.
A chicken soup awaits me there
A soup beyond reproach – a rare
Prime beefsteak in Madeira sauce,
A Goulash (evergreen resource!)
A savoury ragout of venison
A mushroom omelette, and the benison
Of luscious *Kipfelkoch* to follow,
Then gateau... and I feel less hollow.
Two pints of beer – I do not ask
A lot to drink at lunch – a flask
Of vintage Gumpolds, not too cold,

# *Austrian* cooking

And vermouths, three or four all told.
Then, in the cause of good digestion,
A long cigar's the best suggestion.
I lean well back and scan the ceiling,
My coffee comes (and a nice full feeling).
So home — and there I must have peace,
From worldly cares to seek surcease
From two till four, and, stretched my length
Beneath the bedclothes, gather strength.
For tea I saunter into town
And scan the menus up and down
For knuckle end of pork — a dish
I'm partial to — a scrap of fish,
Cold gosling and a bite of cheese.
I'm really quite content with these,
For gourmets rigorously exclude,
So early, any *heating* food.
Dinner's upon us! Now I make
A *light* meal, for my stomach's sake.
Some brains in aspic, fricassée
Of veal, and tongue suffice for me...
And meat loaf.... Or I might enjoy
Smoked pork and cabbage, or would toy
With rumpsteak and a nice savoy,
And only later, 'pon my soul,
Take with the wine a garnished roll.
And now I think you will see why
Good food admits no other tie:
Because I've nothing else, you see
Life looks uncommon good to me...

*(Translated from the Viennese by John Trench)*

# By Way of a Summary

# *Austrian* cooking

## Soups and their Garnishes

Bread Soup (*Panadlsuppe*), 21
Butter Dumplings, Small
  (*Butternockerl*), 10
Calf's Head Soup (*Kalbskopfsuppe*), 17
Caraway Soup (*Kuemmelsuppe*), 20
Cauliflower Soup (*Karfiolsuppe*), 22
Cheese Slices (*Kaeseschnitten*), 10
Clear Broth Soup (*Klare Rindsuppe*), 6
Cream of Game Soup
  (*Wildpureesuppe*), 20
Cream of Lentil Soup
  (*Linsenpureesuppe*), 19
Eingetropftes, 10
Fried Peas (*Backerbsen*), 9
Goulash Soup (*Gulasch Suppe*), 16
Leberreis, 12
'Little Patches' (*Fleckerl*), 15
Liver Dumplings (*Lebernoedel*), 11
  Small (*Lebernocerln*), 11
Marrow Dumplings, Small
  (*Mark Knoederl*), 13
Meat Turnovers (*Schlick Krapfen*), 14
Mushroom Soup
  (*Schwammerlsuppe*), 25
Noodles for Soup (*Suppenudeln*), 14
Pasta Squares, Small (*Fleckerl*), 15
Potato Soup (*Erdaepfelsuppe*), 21
Reibgerstl, 13
Savoury Squares (*Biscuit Schoeberl*), 9
Savoury Strudel (*Lungenstrudel*), 12
Savoy Cabbage Soup
  (*Kohlminestrasuppe*), 23
Semolina Dumplings,
  Small (*Griessnockerl*), 13
Semolina Soup
  (*Geroestete Griess Suppe*), 22

Soup made with Roe
  (*Fischbeuschelsuppe*), 16
Soup made with Split Peas
  (*Erbsenpureesuppe*), 18
Sour Cream Soup (*Stoss Suppe*), 23
To Clear Soup, 8
Tomato Soup (*Paradeis Suppe*), 24
Vegetable Soup (*Fruelingssuppe*), 15

## Fish

Carp in Aspic (*Gesulzter Karpfen*), 28
  in Paprika Sauce
    (*Gesulzter Paprikakarpfen*), 29
  with Sour Cream
    (*Karpfen mit Rahm*), 30
Eel with Parsley (*Gebratener Aal*), 28
Fish Cooked in Brown Ale
  (*Schwarzfisch*), 31
  in Marinade
    (*Marienerte Bratfische*), 31
Pike, with Anchovy Butter
  (*Hecht mit Sardellenbutter*), 30
  Baked (*Gebratener Hecht*), 29
  in Cream Sauce
    (*Gespickter Hecht*), 29

## Meat, Game and Poultry

Aspic Jelly (*Aspik*), 56
Beef, Boiled (*Gekochtes Rindfleisch*), 39
  Goulash (*Rindsgulasch*), 40
  Marinated (*Sauerbraten*), 41
  Paprika (*Paprika Rostbraten*), 39
  Pot Roast, Stuffed with Frankfurters
    (*Wuerstelbraten*), 42
Brains in Egg and Breadcrumbs
  (*Gebackenes Hirn*), 46

# Index

Brawn (*Haussulz*), 59
*Bruckfleisch*, 43
Calf's Head, Fried
    (*Gebackener Kalbskop*), 47
Calf's Liver, Fried
    (*Gebackene Kalbsleber*), 47
Calves' Brains, Roulade Filled
    with (*Hirnroulade*), 48
Chicken Livers, Pâté of
    (*Huehnerleberpastete*), 61
Chicken, Fried Spring (*Backhendl*), 53
    Galantine of (*Huehnergalantine*), 60
    Paprika (*Paprikahendl*), 54
    Stuffed (*Gefueltes Huhn*), 58
Green Peppers, Stuffed
    (*Gefuellte Paprika*), 51
*G'roestl*, 52
*G'roestl*, Tiroler, 52
Ham Cornets (*Schinkenstanitzl*), 62
Ham Roll (*Schinkencremeroulade*), 55
Hare, Saddle of, in Cream Sauce
    (*Hasenbraten mit Rahmsauce*), 52
*Katzenjammer*, 62
Kidneys with Onions
    (*Geroestete Nieren*), 48
Lights (*Beuschel*), 46
*Liptauer*, 63
Liver, Tyrolean (*Tyroler Leber*), 50
*Matrosenfleisch*, 39
Mutton Stew, Styrian
    (*Steirisches Schopsernes*), 45
*Naturschnitzel*, 37
Pariser Schnitzel, 38
Pork, with Horseradish (*Krenfleisch*), 44
    Roast (*Schweinsbraten*), 44
    Roast, with Cream Sauce
    (*Jungfernbraten mit Rahmsauce*), 43
    with Sauerkraut (*Krautfleisch*), 45
Potato Goulash (*Erdaepfelgulasch*), 50

Roast Mince (*Faschierter Braten*), 49
Steak à la Esterhazy
    (*Esterhazy Rostbraten*), 38
Steak à la Viennoise
    (*Wiener Rostbraten*), 42
Veal, Boned Knuckle of
    (*Kalbsvoegerl*), 36
    Escalopes in Cream Sauce
    (*Rahmscnitzel*), 37
    Goulash (*Kalbsgulasch*), 35
    Ragout (*Eigenmachtes Kalbpleisch*), 33
    Roast Knuckle of
    (*Gebratene Kalbsstelze*), 34
    Stuffed Breast of
    (*Gefuellte Kalbsbrust*), 34
Venison, Leg and Loin of,
    in Cream Sauce
    (*Rehbraten mit Rahmsauce*), 53
*Wiener Schnitzel*, 36

## Vegetables

Brown Lentils (*Braune Linsen*), 66
Cabbage, Red or White
    (*Geduenstetes Kraut*), 67
    Savoy, Viennese Style (*Kohl*), 73
Carrots (*Karotten*), 68
    with Garden Peas
    (*Karotten mit Gruenen Erbsen*), 69
Cos Lettuce with Green Peas
    (*Kochsalat mit Gruenen Erbsen*), 70
French Beans in Cream Sauce
    (*Gruene Fisolen*), 68
'*G'roeste*', 70
Marrow (*Kuerbiskraut*), 71
Mushroom Soufflé
    (*Schwammerlsoufflee*), 74
Potato Slices (*Erdaepfelschnitten*), 69

# *Austrian* cooking

Purée of Dried Yellow Peas
   (*Erbsenpuree*), 66
Rice (*Reis*), 71
Risi Bisi, 72
*Sauerkraut,* 73

## Salads

Cabbage Salad (*Krautsalat*), 77
   Warm (*Warmer Krautsalat*), 78
Cucumber Salad (*Gurkensalat*), 77
Mushroom Salad
   (*Schwammerlsalat*), 80
Potato Mayonnaise
   (*Mayonnaise Salat*), 79

## Savoury Sauces

Anchovy Sauce I
   (*Sardellensauce I*), 85
Anchovy Sauce II
   (*Sardellensauce II*), 86
Boiled Beef, Sauce for
   (*Warme Rindpleisch Sauce*), 87
Caper Sauce (*Kapernsauce*), 84
Chives Sauce (*Schnittlauch Sauce*), 86
Cranberry Sauce (*Preiselbeersauce*), 85
Dill Sauce (*Dillensauce*), 82
Dried Beans, Sauce made with
   (*Bohnensauce*), 82
Hard-boiled Egg Yolks,
   Sauce made with, 82
Horseradish Sauce I (*Krensauce*), 83
Horseradish Sauce II (*Mandelkren*), 83
   with Vinegar Dressing (*Essig Kren*), 83
Mushroom Sauce
   (*Schwammerlsauce*), 86

Onion Sauce (*Zwiebelsauce*), 87
Tomato Sauce (*Paradeis Sauce*), 84

## Dumplings and the Like

Bread Dumplings I
   (*Semmelknoedel*), 93
Dumpling Cooked in a Napkin
   (*Serviettenknoedel*), 94
Dumplings made with Breadcrumbs
   (*Broeselknoedel*), 90
Fried Meat Turnovers
   (*Zillertaler Krapfen*), 94-5
Meat Dumplings (*Fleischknoedel*), 91
*Nockerl,* 90
Pasta and Ham (*Schinkenfleckerl*), 92
Poor Knights filled with Calves Brains
   (*Hirnpofesen*), 92-3
Semolina Dumplings
   (*Greissknoedel*), 91

## Desserts, Hot and Cold, Including Sweet Sauces

Almond Pudding
   (*Mandel Pudding*), 122-3
Apple Snow (*Apfelschnee*), 97
Apricot Dumplings
   (*Marillenknoedel*), 104
Bohemian Bun Pudding
   (*Dampfnudeln*), 101
Bread Pudding (*Scheiterhaufen*), 107
'Canaries Milk' (*Kananrienmilch*), 101
Cherry Dessert
   (*Kirschenmehlspeise*), 103
Chestnut Mont Blanc
   (*Kastanienreis*), 102

Chocolate Pudding
(*Schokolade Pudding*), 125
Chocolate Sauce
(*Schokolade Sauce*), 121
with Whipped Cream, 125
Coffee Pudding (*Kaffeepudding*), 122
Cream Cheese Turn-overs
(*Topfentascherl*), 114
Cream Pudding (*Creme Pudding*), 98
Croissants, Pudding made with
(*Kipfelkoch*), 103
Floating Islands (*Scheenockerl*), 112-3
'Fried Mice' (*Gebackene Maeuse*), 99
'Fried Straw' (*Gebackenes Stroh*), 99
*Griess Schmarrn*, 111
Hazel Nut and Rum Sauce, 122
Hazel Nut Cream
(*Haselnuss Creme*), 103
Hazel Nut Pudding
(*Haselnuss Pudding*), 121
with Hazel Nut Cream
(*Haselnussauflauf mit Creme*), 102
*Kaiserschmarrn*, 110
*Kalter Reis*, 100
'Ladies' Soufflé' (*Damen Auflauf*), 118
Lemon Soufflé (*Zitronen Auflauf*), 120
'Locksmith's Apprentices',
(*Schlosserbuben*), 109
*Mohr Im Hemd*, 123
*Nuss Nudeln*, 105
Nut Pudding (*Nusspudding*), 124
Pancakes (*Palatschinken*), 105
Pancakes, Baked, with Vanilla Cream
(*Cremepalatschinken*), 97
Plum Dumplings
(*Zwetschkenknoedel*), 117
'Poor Knights', (*Pofesen*), 106
Prune Fritters, (*Schlossenbuben*), 109

Rice Pudding (*Reisauflauf*), 106
Rolls, Pudding made with
(*Semmel Auflauf*), 113
Rum Pudding (*Rum Pudding*), 124
Rum Sauce, 125
*Salzburger Nockerl*, 108
*Schmarrn*, 109
Semolina Cake Served as a Sweet
(*Greisstorte als Mehlspeise*), 100
Snowballs (*Schneeballen*), 112
Soufflé Dish, To Prepare a, 118
Soufflé Rothschild, 119
Sponge Fingers and Wine, Pudding
made with (*Biskotten Auflauf*), 98
Steamed Puddings, 120
Stephanie Omelette, 114
Strawberry Soufflé (*Erdbeer Auflauf*), 119
Vanilla Cream (*Vanille Creme*), 115
Vanilla Custard (*Kananrienmilch*), 101
'Viennese Pudding'
(*Wiener Koch*), 116-7
White Wine Sauce, 123
Wine Pudding (*Weinkoch*), 116
Yellow Pudding with Chocolate Sauce
(*Gelber Pudding mit Schokolade
Sauce*), 121

## *Cakes, Pastries and Biscuits*

Almond 'Bread' (*Mandelbrot*), 144
Almond Kisses (*Mandel Busserl*), 145
Almond Slices (*Mandelschnitten*), 144
Apple Flan (*Apfel Pastete*), 128
Apple Slices (*Apfelschnitten*), 128
Apple Strudel (*Apfelstrudel*), 129
Apricot Strudel (*Marillenstrudel*), 148
'Bee's Sting' (*Bienenstich*), 130

# $\mathscr{Austrian}$ cooking

Biscuits I (*Teebaekerei I*), 160
Biscuits II (*Teebaekerei II*), 160
Bishop's Bread I (*Bischofsbrot I*), 129
Bishop's Bread II (*Bischofsbrot II*), 130
Brandy Rings (*Cognac Ringerl*), 135
*Buchteln*, 168
Butter Rings (*Butter Ringerl*), 136
Carnival Doughnuts
    (*Faschingskrapfen*), 169
Cheese Biscuits (*Kaesebaekerei*), 166
Cherry Strudel (*Kirschenstrudel*), 148
Chestnut Slices (*Kastanienschnitten*), 141
'Children's Rusks' (*Kinderwieback*), 142
Children's Teacake (*Kinderwieback*), 142
Chocolate Fondant Biscuits
    (*Schokolade Fondant*), 156
Chocolate Kisses
    (*Schokolade Busserl*), 155
Chocolate Roll (*Schokolade Roulade*), 158
'Chocolate Sausage'
    (*Schokoladewurst*), 157
Chocolate Slices
    (*Schokoladeschnitten*), 156
Cinnamon Stars (*Zimtsterne*), 165
Cornets (*Stanitzl*), 158
Cream Cheese Crescents
    (*Topfenkipferl*), 162
Cream Cheese Pastries
    (*Topfengolatschen*), 188
Cream Cheese Slices
    (*Topfenschnitten*), 161
Cream Filling I, 133
Cream Filling II, 133
Cream Slices (*Cremeschnitten*), 133
Crescents (*Kipferl aus Zuckerteig*), 143
Croissants (*Butterkipferl*), 183
    with Marzipan Filling
    (*Butterkipferl au Chevalier*), 183
'English Bread' (*Englisches Brot*), 134

Filled Honeycakes
    (*Gefuellte Lebkuchen*), 138
Florentines (*Florentiner*), 137
Fruit Loaves (*Fruechtenbrot*), 189
*Gerstnerkrapfen*, 139
*Gleichheitskuchen*, 139
Guglhupf à la Sacher
    (*Sacher Guglhupf* ), 155
Guglhupf aus Germteig I, 171
Guglhupf aus Germteig II, 172
Guglhupf made with Baking Powder
    (*Guglhupf mit Backpulver*), 134
    made with Cream
    (*Rahmguglhupf*), 148
Gipsy Slices (*Zigeunerschnitten*), 164
Ham Biscuits (*Schinkenbaekerei*), 166
Hazel Nut Biscuits
    (*Haselnuss Baeckerei*), 136
Hazel Nut Rolls (*Haselnuss Rollen*), 184
Hazel Nut Sticks
    (*Haselnuss Stengerl*), 137
'Hedgehogs' (*Igel*), 142
Honey Biscuits (*Lebzelt Baekerei*), 147
*Husarenkrapfel*, 140
Ischl Tartlets (*Ischler Krapfen*), 141
Jam Envelopes (*Polsterzipfel*), 152
Linzer Slices (*Linzerschnitten*), 143
Marzipan Crescents
    (*Marzipan Kipferl*), 184
Morello Cherry Cake
    (*Weichselkuchen*), 163
*Nusspotitze*, 177
Nut Boats (*Nuss Schipperl*), 152
Nut Crescents (*Nussbeugel*), 175
Nut Ring (*Nusskranz*), 186
Nut Roll (*Nuss Roulade*), 151
Nut Strudel made with Yeast
    (*Nuss Strudel*), 178

Pariser Creme, 165
Pastry Slices (*Muerbe Schnitten*), 150
Plaited Coffee Loaf (*Kaffeestriezel*), 174
Plum Cake made with Yeast
    (*Zwetschkenkuchen*), 180
Poppyseed Crescents
    (*Mohnbeugel*), 176
Poppyseed Strudel made with Yeast
    (*Mohnstrudel*), 179
Puff Pastry (*Blaetterteig*), 131-2
Puff Pastry made with Cream Cheese
    (*Topfenblaetterteig*), 161
Puff Pastry made with Yeast I
    (*Germbutterteig I*), 181
Puff Pastry made with Yeast II
    (*Germbutterteig II*), 182
Raisin or Sultana Bread
    (*Milchbrot*), 173
'Rascals' (*Spitzbuben*), 157
Redcurrant Flan (*Ribisel Kuchen*), 154
Ring Cake (*Kranzkuchen*), 185
Rose Cakes (*Rosenkrapfen*), 154
'Saddle of Venison Gateau'
    (*Rehruecken*), 153
'Snails' (*Schnecken*), 187
Sour Cream Strudel
    (*Milchrahmstrudel*), 149
Strudel Paste (*Strudelteig*), 159
Vanilla Crescents (*Vanillekipferl*), 162
Widow's Kisses (*Witwenkuesse*), 164
Yeast, 167
*Zaunerstollen*, 163

## *Gateaux and Icings*

*Alpenbuttertorte*, 193
*Biskottentorte*, 194
Chestnut Gateau I

(*Kastanientorte I*), 202
Chestnut Gateau II
    (*Kastanientorte II*), 202
Chocolate Gateau with Almonds I
    (*Schokoladetorte mit
    Mandeln I*), 214
Chocolate Gateau with Almonds II
    (*Schokoladetorte mit
    Mandeln II*), 215
Coffee Cream Gateau I
    (*Kaffeecremetorte I*), 200
Coffee Cream Gateau II
    (*Kaffeecremetorte II*), 201
Cream Cheese Gateau
    (*Topfentorte*), 214
Cream Gateau (*Cremetorte*), 195
Dobos Torte, 199
Easter Gateau (*Ostertorte*), 208
Hazel Nut Gateau I
    (*Haselnusstorte I*), 199
Hazel Nut Gateau II
    (*Haselnusstorte II*), 199
Kathi's Special Roulade, 192
Linzertorte, 203
    creamed method (*Geruehrte
    Linzertorte*), 204
Marbled Cream Slab
    (*Bunter Rehruecken*), 194
Meran Gateau
    (*Meraner Torte*), 204
Morello Cherry Gateau
    (*Weichselcremetorte*), 216
*Muerbe Torte I*, 205
*Muerbe Torte II*, 205
Nut Gateau (*Nusstorte*), 206
Orange Gateau
    (*Orangentorte*), 206
Panamatorte, 207

# *Austrian* cooking

Paulinentorte, 211
Pischinger Torte, 210
Punch Gateau (*Punsch Torte*), 210
Sachertorte, 212
Semolina Cake (*Griess Torte*), 199
Soft Chocolate Gateau
    (*Weiche Schokoladetorte*), 217
Strawberry Gateau
    (*Erdbeerkuchen*), 198
Traunkirchner Torte, 215
White Almond Cake
    (*Weisse Mandeltorte*), 217
Whitsun Gateau (*Pfingsttorte*), 209
Zebra Gateau (*Zebra Torte*), 218

## Notes

# *Notes*

# *Notes*

# *Notes*

# Notes

# *Notes*

## Notes

# Notes

*Notes*

*Notes*

# *Notes*

## Notes

*Notes*

# Notes